A Countryman's Woods

A Countryman's Woods

by Hal Borland ❧ photographs by Les Line

ALFRED A. KNOPF   NEW YORK   1983

This is a Borzoi Book
Published by Alfred A. Knopf, Inc.

Library of Congress Cataloging in Publication Data

Borland, Hal. [date].
A countryman's woods.

Includes index.
1. Trees—United States—Addresses, essays, lectures.
2. Forest flora—United States—Addresses, essays, lectures.
I. Line, Les.   II. Title.
QK482.B68 1983   582.160973   83–47943
ISBN 0–394–52724–0

Manufactured in the United States of America
First Edition

For Barbara and for Lois

Contents

Foreword

America is traditionally a land of trees, though there are large areas of the West and Southwest where the only native trees are stunted willows along the seasonal watercourses. When the first Europeans reached the New England shores they found "boundless woodland" reaching inland. The first of them to go up the Hudson River encountered white pines more than a hundred feet tall along both shores and inland as far as they could see. The first settlers reported this to be "a land of unbroken woodland reaching westward."

These reports can be taken with a grain of salt. They were made by people who came from an England and a France that had been without virgin woodlands for several generations. They also were people who did not venture far inland when they first reached these shores. Other reports were made by such explorers as Giovanni da Verrazano, who in 1524 made an expedition from Narragansett Bay as far inland as what is now central New York state. Verrazano reported "open plains twenty-five or thirty leagues in extent, entirely free of trees or other hindrances." Other explorers who traveled inland told much the same story. And eventually the pioneers themselves found they did not have to hew their way, yard by yard, through unbroken woodland from the Massachusetts coast to the open prairies of Illinois.

This was, truly, a wooded land, at least the eastern half of the continent. But the big woods had openings, some natural, some created by men. The eastern Indians were farmers, basically. They made clearings for their fields of corn, beans, and squash. When they had exhausted the natural fertility of one field, they girdled and burned trees to make another clearing. And they burned brushland to encourage grass. That was one way to create more forest margin, which was where the birds and animals they relied on for meat and leather preferred to feed. Few game animals ever lived in the deep woods, which were dark and grassless.

There are few virgin woodlands left today, and most of them are in remote areas. The forests we know best, those accessible to most of us, are relatively young and full of clearings. In Connecticut, for example, a survey made in the mid-1940s showed that 90 percent of the woodlands in the state were less than sixty years old. This is a cut-over land. But it certainly is not without woods, young though they may be. In 1860 only 27 percent of Connecticut was wooded. This probably was less than half, perhaps only one-third, of the wooded area this state had when the first white settlers came. But by 1910, Connecticut's woodlands had expanded to cover 45 percent of the state; and by 1955 some 63 percent of the state was in forest again, despite the vast increase in population and the sprawling spread of cities and their suburbs.

Other New England states never were as extensively cleared of trees as Connecticut. No more than 25 percent of Maine, for instance, ever was cleared. And today, despite all the tree-cutting of the past, about three-quarters of New England is wooded, probably not a great deal less than was in timber when the Europeans arrived here to stay.

I can read human history whenever I walk through the woods in my area. Most of these woodlands have networks of old stone walls, many now tumbled into serpentine stone piles. Those walls were not laid up by woodcutters taking out sawlogs or firewood or wood for charcoal. They were built by farmers who had cut the original trees to clear fields and were waging war against the stony freight brought here by the glaciers. They cleared the stones from their fields year after year and built walls not only to mark boundaries but to dispose of those stones and make way for the plow. On my own mountainside are half a dozen such wall-enclosed fields, now grown up with trees probably close to a hundred years old, fields that haven't been tilled since the days of ox-drawn plows. Now they are a part of the woodland that covers the whole mountainside.

Like most of this area, that mountainside has been cut over several times. Those wall-enclosed fields, now gone back to woods, are reminders of the first cutting, which was to clear land for the plow. Many of the original farmers were succeeded by their sons, but after two—or at most three—generations, the thin soil up there was "farmed out" or washed away. The upland farmers died, or went West, or moved down to the lowlands, following their own eroded soil. The upland fields were abandoned and reclaimed by second-growth timber.

Eventually those fields became woodlots, where the lowland farmers cut firewood and a few sawlogs. Then the iron industry got a start in this area, which had iron ore and limestone. For fuel, the industry needed charcoal, and here were these hills covered with second-growth timber. So again the trees were cut, to make charcoal for the iron furnaces. But eventually the furnaces cooled and the iron industry moved to the source of coal and coke. And once more the woods were allowed to creep back. They grew, and the trees were cut a third time, to be sawed into lumber for houses in the cities and suburbs.

And now the trees have grown again.

On my own mountainside, as on most of the hills of southern and central New England, is a mixture of trees—white pines, hemlocks, oaks, white ash, hickories, birch. There is less beech in my woods than I would like, and fewer maples (my maples grow down in the valley). There is more gray birch, and less white birch, than I would choose to have. But this is a volunteer mixture, still in the process of maturing as a woodland.

The farmer who owned this land before World War I did a bit of logging up there. The lumber from which he built the house I now live in was sawed from logs he cut on that mountainside. I still find thirty-inch stumps of old chestnuts up there, stubbornly defying time. The beams, rafters, and interior trim—even the stairway itself—came from those trees. The sheathing and other lumber came from white pines whose stumps have rotted and disappeared. Strangely, it seems to me, two rather large piles of sawdust remain, dark and moldered but most of it identifiably white pine, where the portable sawmill cut planks and boards from the logs.

So I get particular pleasure from this house, which literally grew on that mountainside, and from the woods maturing there today. A part of that pleasure, I am sure, comes from the fact that I grew up in a land of virtually no trees, the High Plains of eastern Colorado. My father, who grew up among the trees of eastern Nebraska, missed them so much that he bought seedling cottonwoods, believed to be the trees most likely to grow in that area. He set them out, watered them, and watched them take root and grow all summer. That winter the jackrabbits not only girdled them; they ate the stems like so much macaroni. The next spring new seedlings sprouted from the roots, but it was a dry summer and by mid-July they simply curled up and quit. Father gave up, too, and learned to live without trees. And I was grown before I lived in a timbered land. Perhaps that is why the trees on my own mountainside are so precious to me now. Perhaps that is why I am writing this book.

This is not intended to be a treatise on trees, nor is it a scientific study of them. It is a book *about* trees, yes. It has basic botanical information, as simplified as I can make it. But mostly it is a kind of *celebration* of trees. I have expanded the scope a bit to include some shrubs and vines, those which belong with the trees, making it a book about the woodland. And I have written primarily about the woodland of northeastern North America, though a few times I have broadened my license to discuss special trees I have known elsewhere, because merely mentioning them brings back special memories.

It is that kind of book, insistently personal. And Les Line's pictures are almost as free from regional inhibitions. He comes from Michigan, and he has his own special memories.

We hope you like our trees, and we hope you will go to the handbooks to learn still more about them.

H A L   B O R L A N D

Photographer's Note

Spring came unheralded, that year of 1978, to the banks of the Housatonic River a short piece down the road from the Connecticut–Massachusetts line and the marble knolls of Bartholomew's Cobble. Male red-winged blackbirds staked out nesting territories in the willows and cattails with flashing epaulets and bubbling song. Peepers, emerging from long hibernation, announced the thawing of the marsh with a clamorous chorus. Crimson flames of millions of tiny flowers outlined every branch and twig of the red maples over in the swamp. On the sun-warmed hillside, delicate purple flowers of hepatica waved above the previous fall's decaying leaves.

These and many other ordinary, yet extraordinary, events of this time of annual renewal passed without celebration for the first time in thirty-five years. In a frame farmhouse by the river, in a cramped study overlooking gnarled apple trees, a greening pasture, and, beyond, a Berkshire mountainside once again come to life, a typewriter stood silent.

Hal Borland, naturalist and novelist, one of America's most beloved nature essayists, had died in winter's waning days, before pussy willows and muddy roads and freshets from the hill and marsh-marigolds in the bog signaled the renaissance of March.

He was widely known as a chronicler of the New England seasons, but Hal Borland's youth was spent far west of his adopted Berkshires. His birthplace was the valley of the Nemaha River in southeastern Nebraska, and he told of those formative years in his first story for my magazine, *Audubon*, having been asked over the phone, without warning, by an editor he had never met or talked with, to become a regular contributor to a publication for which he had never written.

"In the early days my father built a dam on the Nemaha, and a mill to grind corn and saw lumber," he wrote. "But by the time of my boyhood the wooded hills of its watershed had been stripped and cropped and cornfields were creeping down onto its floodplain. Only a few people, like Grandma, knew and cherished its looping channel and the tangles, brier patches, thickets, and groves that persisted in its valley.

"There were two grandmothers, but the other one was a widow—starchy, reserved, and critical. She distrusted sunlight, which faded her carpets. She insisted nature belonged outdoors and didn't think much of it even there. She was Grand*mother*, capitalized, formal.

"Grand*ma*, on the other hand, was slippery elm bark and cherry-sap gum, dandelion greens and sassafras tea. I think of her every time I smell black walnut hulls; which is one reason we go out every autumn, here in our Connecticut Berkshires, and gather a few pecks of butternuts and hickory nuts, and try to beat the squirrels to a few handfuls of hazelnuts, though we seldom succeed."

Growing-up time was spent on the High Plains of eastern Colorado, where Hal's father became a small-town newspaper editor. Those were the years "when the Old West was passing and the New West was emerging. It was a time when we still heard echoes and already saw shadows, on moonlit nights when the coyotes yapped on the hilltops, and on hot summer afternoons when mirages shimmered, dust devils spun across the flats, and towering cumulus clouds sailed like galleons across the vast blueness of the sky. Echoes of remembrance of what men once did there, and visions of what they would do tomorrow."

For a country editor's boy, a career in journalism was a natural choice. Eventually Hal Borland came to the staff of the *New York Times*, and one morning in 1941 he submitted a short essay on oak trees to the editorial page. A Hal Borland nature editorial soon became a fixture in the Sunday paper. The last of 1,750 appeared the day before his death.

Most, from the mid-1940s on, were written from that upstairs room, shaded from the sun by a Norway spruce of remarkable shape and proportions, in that farmhouse along the Housatonic. For this son of the prairie and plain had found, in the Berkshires, "the perfect world, a home at the end of nowhere. This is the only way to live, waiting for the vernal equinox, seeing an apple tree blossom, or coming on an old coon and her kits fishing for clams late at night."

He was an intensely private man. There was no name on the mailbox in front of the Borland farm, and few of the many people who traveled the curving road along the Housatonic on their way to the fabled Cobble reservation knew they had passed the home of a famous author whose work they loved. He made few public appearances, eschewed the company of his literary peers, asked for no idolization from his readers. In the ten years I knew Hal Borland—as his editor, co-author, friend, and regular correspondent—he made only two visits to New York City, one to screen a movie based on his best-selling novel about an Indian lad, *When the Legends Die*; and the second to receive the prestigious John Burroughs Medal. He simply hated to leave his farm and river and mountain, especially for the city, and he found few compelling reasons to do so.

This book and its companion, *A Countryman's Flowers*, were conceived one warm afternoon in late April as Hal and I looked for a patch of hepaticas on the hillside above his home. We found them, of course, right where he had first discovered their fuzzy liver-shaped leaves and variable blossoms, ranging from a faintly tinted white to the densest purple you can imagine, twenty-five years before.

Just about the first thing we decided was that these two books would not be guides in any sense of the word. There are an ample number of volumes—some fairly easy for the layman to use, others requiring a botanist's bent, if not a degree—to help people identify specific wildflowers and trees. (The shrubs, however, could stand a good deal more attention. Perhaps this is because even the professionals get confused on occasion and have a hard time naming some of the shrubs.)

Celebration was the word Hal had in mind, and it is a good one. To celebrate, the dictionaries tell us, means to honor, to proclaim, to portray in poetic form, to contribute to public awareness or enjoyment. And that Hal surely does, while passing along just the right prescription of solid botanical knowledge.

For my part, I have tried through my photographs to capture the *essence*, the soul of each particular tree or shrub. I have not composed pictures to aid the reader in identifying these eighty-plus species, for that is best done with botanical keys and detailed drawings of various tree parts, though some of the pictures surely could help in that quest. Rather, I hope these images will lead to discovery, to understanding, as the process of gathering them did for me.

The reader will find, then, photographs of leaves—but not always the perfect leaves that artists illustrate in field guides, for leaves seldom are perfect in nature. They become perforated by worms, covered with insect galls, fall to the forest floor in October winds and rains and quickly lose their bright autumn colors. There are buds and flowers, berries and nuts, branches and bark. The besieged American elm is portrayed as one commonly sees it today—a lifeless skeleton, this one in the "yard" of an abandoned shack in Down East Maine, a long-ago victim of deadly blight but too sturdy and too proud to crumble. So, too, is the American chestnut shown—a great snag reaching toward a stormy sky over the Blue Ridge Mountains of Virginia. And the black spruce chosen is one I know well, a squat tree in a vast sphagnum bog near the coast of Maine where I go to find grass-pink orchids and pitcher plants in July.

(To answer the questions of the photographers in our audience: All of the pictures were taken with single-lens reflex cameras, many of them with Minolta's exceptional X-700 system. A variety of lenses were used, from a 24mm wide-angle to a 400mm telephoto, but most especially a 100mm macro lens. Kodachrome 64 was my exclusive choice of film. Although I prefer to work in natural light, however dim, on a few occasions the use of flash was unavoidable; Minolta's autoflash metering system made it painless, eliminating laborious exposure calculations. Always the camera was hand-held; the students in my nature photography classes know well my aversion to tripods.)

The order in which trees and shrubs appear in this book closely follows current thinking as to plant evolution and family relationships. Thus we begin with the conifers, which evolved before the flowering plants. And the first conifer, though it may not look like one, is the ginkgo or maidenhair tree from China, a true living fossil that is widely planted in North America. The hardwoods are arranged with the most primitive trees first. And, of course, trees of a kind are grouped together—the birches, the maples, the beech family (including the oaks), the rose family, and so on.

That Hal Borland did not live to see these books published grieves me, and the fault is wholly mine. Hal never missed a copy deadline by even a day, and as an editor I can say that of far too few writers. The text for *A Countryman's Flowers* and *A Countryman's Woods* was promptly finished. The pictures came together in a trickle. Bad weather, magazine deadlines, affairs that seemed more urgent canceled too many planned photographic expeditions to Borland Country. I guess I believed this man was immortal. Not until the fall of 1977, when the Line family bought its own year-round retreat on the New York side of the Berkshires, did the picture-taking begin in earnest. For Borland fans, however, this one last book of new essays will be like discovering a forgotten jar of maple syrup in a cupboard corner, or finding a butternut tree you did not know grew in the back-forty woodlot.

Hal was responsible for the initial choice of trees and shrubs to feature on these pages. But he always intended to write additional essays should I take pictures of important or particularly attractive species he had over-looked. You will find, therefore, a few essays herein with my own initials at the end, pieces Hal would have written had he lived to see the project completed. If his spirit flows freely from my words, do not be surprised, for my life and work were influenced by this countryman even before we met, when I first read a book of his. (At the corner of my desk lies a battered, black bison horn. A country editor's boy found it one hot summer afternoon while exploring the Colorado plains, long after the last buffalo herd had passed. He kept it within reach in that study below the forested Berkshire hills, a tangible memory of a youth spent in a world without such magnificent trees. And one day I shall pass it on, to a naturalist who will celebrate the world around us in the Borland tradition.)

No epitaph was chiseled in stone for my countryman friend. But I come back to words once appended to his biography in *Who's Who in America*:

"I am a fortunate man. I grew up on a frontier, escaped early success, had things to say when I matured. I have been able to make a living at work I wanted to do, to write what I believed and find an audience. My purpose has been to write at least a few paragraphs that will be remembered after I am dead."

More than a few paragraphs, Hal.

L E S   L I N E
Amenia, New York
January 1983

xvii

The Woodland Year

Bud, Blossom, and Leaf

I see the first signs of spring along the riverbank, in the willows and the red-osier dogwoods. When the temperature gets well into the forties and stays there a few days, usually in late March or early April, the red-osier stems, dull red all winter, quicken as though they were pulsing with blood as red as that in my own veins. And the willows have a fresh, alive look in all their amber stems. I am especially aware of this when there is snow on the ground, I admit; then the contrast is eye-catching. But it is still there without the snow.

When I see the red-osiers gleam with life I go up the mountain to a little bog at the head of Middle Brook. Alders grow in that bog, and I will find the male catkins opening. Those catkins have been present all winter, but now they open just enough to release a little pollen because a few female blossoms may be opening. And there I will see my first honeybee, from one of the wild colonies in the hollow trees. I watch the first bees and wonder how they knew the alder catkins would be opening now.

After that, almost anything can happen. Spring can come, or another snowstorm. But when the willows liven and the red-osier dogwoods blush, the red-winged blackbirds may arrive tomorrow, pussy willows may pop their bud scales tonight, and by next week we may have robins and dog-tooth violets. After that we certainly will have shadblow in bloom and swamp maples turning the lowlands scarlet, first with their blossoms, then with their first cautious leaves.

Who can draw up a calendar of woodland spring accurate within ten days? I can't. Spicebush, with its haze of golden-yellow bloom, will come soon now. The elms may already have blossomed, their flowering so insignificant it goes almost unnoticed. I am made aware of elm blossoms by the shower of bud scales; I don't notice them here in the country, but when I go to the village I see them in rifts and windrows along the gutters. And that makes me wonder if we don't actually have a greater fall of leaf scales from the trees in spring than of leaves themselves in the fall. The scales are small, few of them as much as a quarter of an inch across, and they lack the brilliant colors of our October leaves, but they fall by the countless billions in April and May and add to the woodland's humus.

Sugar maples come to bloom rather late, and because their flowers are green and yellow they easily pass unnoticed. So do the blossoms on the ash trees, which ripen into samaras, seeds with vanes of tan tissue that provide wings to carry them to a new and possibly hospitable seedbed. The oaks make no showing of their blossoms, though the staminate flowers dangle like greenish-yellow catkins at their twig tips. The big greenish-white blossoms of the tuliptree wait until the leaves are out and well spread.

Meanwhile, here on my own mountainside we have had the spring spectacle of aspens and birches opening leaf buds and slowly unfolding infant leaves as delicately tinted as pastel chiffon. When first out of their buds, those leaves are flesh pink, lemon yellow, palest lavender, with only a hint of the green to come. They are not leaves, really. They are a celebration of what is yet to come, the whole leafy woodland under a summer sky spangled with birds and butterflies.

And somewhere along the way—did you ever try to establish a calendar of spring and say that today thus-and-so happens, tomorrow thus-and-something-else?—somewhere along the way the miracle of the hickory bud is performed. Watch, and you will agree that it must be the result of miracles, for neither man nor nature could pack so much so neatly into so little space.

Here is the bud, on the shagbark hickory, a big bud, about the size of a man's thumb. It wasn't that big two months ago, but it is now: big, fat, and eager to burst. The precise time comes, the day, the hour, the minute, and the bud begins to open, the scales to pull apart. They are not scales, really; they are sheaths, with the texture of fabric. They pull apart, curl back, and other coverings part. Inside are leaves, tightly curled. They begin to unfold, pale green, almost yellow, that big terminal leaf, those four smaller leaflets. And as they unfold they reveal the catkins of a male blossom, two stems of catkins, each with three catkins ready to dangle. And another compound leaf, leaflet by leaflet slowly unfolding.

The miracle of spring, magnified in one example, unmistakable. The bud formed last summer, unharmed by winter, nourished by spring, and now these leaves, these blossoms, ready for the summer's work.

The Green, Green World

Forget the solstice and say that all of June, July, and August are summer, here in the Northeast. By September our year has made its turn toward autumn. We make our own seasonal calendar, and I find that if I watch the woodland the seasons are well defined here.

Spring really ends when the trees are all leafed out and past the pale green and pastel shades. That is when the chlorophyll has been distributed and the leaves have gone to work converting water, air, and sunlight into starch and sugar that the trees can use as food. We call this process photosynthesis, but nobody has found a way to do in a factory what is done in a leaf.

Yet there are all those leaves, all those trees and bushes and plants of every kind, green with chlorophyll, working all day and every day, making the basic food for everyone and everything on Earth. Those creatures that don't eat grass and leaves eat those that do. Rob the Earth of chlorophyll, the green leaf, and you would rob it of all life, eventually. And summer is the season of the green leaf and the blossoms that make the seeds from which grow more plants, more green leaves.

June comes, and ours is so green a world that we quite forget the all but leafless days of January, so warm and beneficent a world that we can't quite remember those zero mornings when the land was white with snow and ice. Now it is June, it is warm, it is summer. Strawberries that bloomed in May are red-ripe and juicy. Apple trees that were white with blossoms and loud with bees a month ago are now all leaves and very green fruit the size of marbles. Robins have found their voices and brown thrashers celebrate morning, afternoon, and evening. The whippoorwill calls at dusk, and his mate has laid her eggs in a nest consisting of three short twigs deposited on the ground under a hemlock tree.

Somebody reported that the average-size oak tree has a million leaves and that they would cover an acre of ground. I wonder what is an average-size oak and who counted the leaves. Someone else says this average oak evaporates 28,000 gallons of water through its leaves from April till October. That is about 187 gallons a day. I wonder who measured it, even while I concede that all those figures may be right. Leaves do miraculous things.

By June all the pinks and faint lilacs of infant leaves have gone and the woodland is unbroken green. But not all the same green, by any means. I still can spot the pines and the hemlocks from down here in the valley. I can pick out the aspens, partly by the color, partly by the twinkle of those fluttery leaves. I know how dark is the green of the white oak leaf, how bright the green of the sugar maple, how yellow the poplar leaf can look in certain light. The woodland wears a Joseph's-coat, but all its colors are green.

And it is an all-leaf woodland now. The shadblow's frosty-white blossoms are gone, the big white butterfly-flowers of the dogwood have flown. The pussytails have faded on the chokecherries, and the locust bloom ripens into green pods. Leaves, no two precisely alike even on a single tree, and countless shapes in the woodland: The heart-shaped leaf of the cottonwood, the lance-head leaf of the beech. The scalloped leaves of the oaks, the sawtoothed leaves of elm and chinkapin and hornbeam. The three-lobed, five-lobed, unforgettable leaves of the maples; the mitten leaves of the sassafras, impartially left- or right-handed. The leaflets on a common stem, adding up to an ash leaf, a locust, a hickory, a walnut, a mountain-ash, a staghorn sumac full of fire for September.

Summer, the green-leaf time, the chlorophylled season when the year's growth is made and another year prepared for. By September the buds for April's blossom and fragile new leaf will be seated on this year's twig with scales and sealing gum to protect it from the winter. June, July, and August, the summer sun, the summer rain, and the woodland clothing the rugged hills, shading the brooks and rivers where clean water flows down onto the lowland.

Color, Nuts, and Firewood

We expect three things from our woodland in the autumn: color, nuts, and firewood. The color is for anyone who takes time to look at the mountainside. The nuts are for the squirrels, with a few left over for us. The firewood is all for us.

There is so much color, and such vivid color, that it overwhelms the adjectives. New Englanders simply refer to it as "the color." The sugar maples turn yellow, sunshine yellow, with now and then a tinge of pink. The swamp maples turn red, almost all the shades of red, so that the valleys are like carmine rivers. The birches and aspens turn golden and coppery. The ashes turn tan—at least the black ashes do. But the white ashes go through that incredible series of colors that range from yellowish-green to blue-tan to greenish-blue to purple, honest-to-God purple, and then to bronze, to tan, and to rust.

The underbrush, the bushes and vines, meanwhile are making their own color carnival. Virginia creeper, which has climbed to the very top of the blighted elms and dead chestnuts, becomes a blazing beacon of scarlet, giving the dead limbs spectacular life again. Poison ivy, bush and vine, turns lemon yellow and peach pink and orange, treacherously beautiful. Bittersweet sheds its leaves and reveals bunches of berries that, after the first hard frost, will split their tan husks and display the bright orange fruit.

Wild grapes festoon tree and bush with purple ripeness. Virgin's bower ripens into old-man's-beard. White stars of wild cucumber become fat, soft-prickled pods like pickles. Spicebush berries are red-ripe and ready to pick for storing. Highbush cranberries are about to be picked for jelly. Sumac takes off its vivid warbonnet and offers fat tufts of sour, red, fuzzy berries.

Acorns ripen on white oaks, sweet as chestnuts, and squirrels hoard them. Hazelnuts ripen, and squirrels hoard them. Hickory nuts and black walnuts ripen, and many Yankees call them walnuts indiscriminately. Butternuts ripen where black walnuts refuse to grow. Squirrels hoard them all, forget where they stowed them, and thus plant new groves. Squirrels can't spell *tree* or read statistics, but they are conservationists and reclamationists.

Late apples ripen and we make jelly. Deer come down at dusk to eat windfalls. Maple seeds sprout and seedlings appear between the rows of late onions in the garden. Native barberry gleams with clusters of long, slim, scarlet berries that have a single seed. Mountain-ash seems to revel in the color of its coral-red berries.

The leaves fall. The nuts are harvested. Birds and beasts fatten, and fruit dries on tree and bush and vine for winter fare.

We go to the woods, look for windfalls and dead trees that will maim live trees if winter storms bring them down. We cut firewood for ourselves. We have burned almost every kind of wood that grows in our woodland, one time or another, but my choice runs to hickory for a back log, oak for a front log, and cedar for kindling—cedar or birch. That is if I want a fire for heat. If I want fragrance as well as heat I choose fruit wood, especially apple. Cedar, too, gives a pleasant odor, but we use cedar mostly for starting a fire or livening it up. Hemlock has a pleasant aroma in the fireplace, but it is full of sparks. Don't burn it without a fire screen in place. Pine does the same thing, but less violently. Maple, any species, gives a mild fragrance and burns slowly. It is first-class heating wood, as are beech and locust and oak.

We cut the firewood and stow it in the woodshed. Any firewood should be covered. One year we left a cord or more of sugar maple in the open, and by the next fall half of it was almost worthless in the fire.

I have found that gray birch, generally regarded as of little use except for kindling, burns well and gives a good deal of heat if used while still green. Dry it and it burns like paper. But my choice of kindling still is cedar or pine.

We never bring more firewood into the house than we expect to use in the next day or two. Bark beetles and other insects often hibernate in the wood in the woodshed, and a day or two of house warmth would rouse them and start trouble. After all, our woodshed is only a few steps from the back door of the house, the way any place in the country should be laid out.

Silhouettes and Fingerprints

Winter strips the broad-leafed trees to their essentials. Now they stand in bare bones, all of them except the pines and spruces and hemlocks, and you can see what stands behind their graceful summer shapes.

That elm against the sky, which in summer is a giant green feather-duster—see how its trunk divides some distance from the ground, and divides again and yet again. It reaches upward, widening like an inverted cone, and all its branches point toward the sky.

Across the way is a scarlet oak. It has a trunk three feet through, and your eyes can follow that trunk to the tip of the tree. But its branches start not ten feet from the ground and reach toward the horizon. Here's a tree as broad as it's tall, and rounded, even in leafless winter, like a great dome.

The black ash is essentially a tapering trunk with whorls of lesser limbs, all reaching upward, a svelt and graceful tree. The white ash, almost in contrast, has a portly shape. Its limbs spread outward and unless it grows in a clump it may be even wider than it is tall. The two species grow together on the steep slope where our Springhouse Brook comes lunging down from the mountain to the pasture.

Maples tend to branch like oaks, but with less spread and more lift. The true maple shape, however, can be seen only in freestanding trees, such as the one near the end of our old barn. It was a seedling no more than ten feet high when we came here. Now it is a tree more than a foot through and perhaps forty feet high, and it has achieved the perfect maple shape, that of an egg on its large end. Its first branches are ten feet from the ground and the central trunk can be followed almost to the top. But not all sugar maples are so simple. More often than not the trunk divides several times.

Down the road is a big, old sycamore that shines as though perpetually frosted, but only in spots, remember. Its trunk divides low and keeps dividing, and it branches out in all directions. And the tupelo, or sour gum, is an equal tangle of branches, but from a central stem; the tupelo is truly a confusion of a tree without its leaves.

15

Of all, I think the most beautiful against the winter sky is the little flowering dogwood with its horizontal limbs that reach skyward at their tips and form a fine lace pattern. The dogwood is a picture tree, winter or summer.

Those winter silhouettes are still a challenge to me. But the bigger challenge is to identify winter trees by their bark. The conifers, of course, carry their own credentials both winter and summer, with the exception of the tamarack. But look at the sugar maple's shaggy bark, which has a tendency to flake, and the red maple's somewhat less shaggy bark. And look at the shagbark hickory's very shaggy bark and flakes so big they actually are plates. See the narrow, confluent ridges of the white ash and the almost identical ridges of the black ash. See the smooth, muscular look of the ironwood, the smooth, gray-mottled look of the beech, and the smooth tan and white and green look of the sycamore where big but thin scales of bark have fallen away to reveal the inner bark.

The winter shapes of naked trees are something like the height, weight, and build of an anonymous person. But the winter bark is like the fingerprint file; it is positive identification, once you know what to look for.

A few trees, but only a very few, hold leaves that will serve as positive identification. An oak full of withered brown leaves is very likely to be a scarlet oak. A sleek-bark tree full of crisp tan leaves probably is a beech. And a tree that holds tassels of light tan, winged seeds all winter undoubtedly is a female boxelder, or ashleaf maple. A big shrub with fuzzy upper branches and big, flame-shaped seed clusters must be staghorn sumac.

The Woodlands

Ginkgo

The ginkgo tree, Darwin said, is a "living fossil." It is the lone survivor of a group of trees that throve during the age of the dinosaurs. Today it is found native only in Japan and China, and it is rare even there. Once it grew here. Now it is planted as an ornamental tree along many American streets.

The ginkgo has small, fan-shaped leaves with a notch in the middle, each leaf several inches long and marked with prominent parallel veins. Because the leaves are the same shape as those of the maidenhair fern, the ginkgo sometimes is called maidenhair tree. It bears staminate and pistillate flowers on separate trees. The staminate flowers are in catkins and the pistillate flowers grow in pairs on long stalks. The fruit is a plumlike berry about an inch in diameter with an almond-shaped stone. It turns pale golden yellow when ripe. The flesh is sweet but has a disagreeable, foetid odor. The Chinese, however, make this into a preserve or bake it, and they eat it as an aid to digestion. The kernel of the pit is also valued as food in China and Japan.

The ginkgo has been made a city tree, in good part because it can tolerate the air pollution common to urban areas. It even seems able to withstand a daily dose of automobile fumes along heavily traveled avenues.

Eastern White Pine

P I N U S   S T R O B U S

The pines are far older than the broad-leafed trees. They first appeared during the Pennsylvanian Period, geologically speaking, about 300 million years ago. The broad-leafed trees did not come until about 165 million years later, in the Cretaceous Period. Now the broad-leafed trees dominate, but we still have about ninety species of pine in North America, the biggest of them, the ponderosa of the West, reaching two hundred feet in height.

The first English explorers who sailed up the Hudson River said that stream was lined for miles with pines a hundred and fifty feet tall and fifteen feet in circumference. Today there probably are not a dozen white pines that big the whole length of the river. The original ones were cut for shipbuilding, for lumber, or merely to clear the land. Huge rafts of pine logs once jammed the lower Hudson, to be sawed for housing in Manhattan. The pale yellow wood is soft, easily worked, and durable.

The white pine is a strikingly beautiful tree when it has a chance to grow naturally. Its dominant number is five, most easily seen when the tree is young. Its long, warm green needles come in bundles of five. It tends to send out five branches a year in a whorl around its central stem. Its cones are five or six inches long, narrowly cylindrical, and chocolate brown; they remain closed and green the first year, ripen, turn brown, relax their scales, and release seeds the second year.

The white pine is relatively swift of growth. A seedling will reach a height of sixty feet and a trunk diameter of twenty-four inches in thirty years in a climate such as we have in northwestern Connecticut. The mature bark is scaly gray with irregular but generally vertical grooves, often marked with white streaks of gum or resin from broken branches.

We sometimes call it pasture pine because its seeds will take root in an abandoned field or pasture and grow among weeds, grass, and lesser trees, eventually shading them all out. Many a stand of white pine has come from one venerable old tree left standing in a farm pasture as shade for the cows.

Bristlecone Pine

PINUS ARISTATA

For a long time the giant sequoias of California were believed to be the oldest living things on Earth. Then someone took a pencil-size core from a warped old bristlecone pine high in the California mountains. That tree was more than a thousand years older than the oldest sequoia.

As trees, the bristlecones are rather sorry specimens. They grow at timberline, around ten thousand feet, are scrawny to start with, and are gnarled by wind and weather. Their windward side is stripped of bark and eroded by blown sand and sleet. Their needles, in bundles of five, are short and tired-looking; they are shed only every fifteen years or so. Their cones are about three inches long, the scales tipped with sharp bristles.

In 1958 the Forest Service established the Schulman Memorial Grove of bristlecones in California's White Mountains, honoring Edmund Schulman, who had believed the bristlecones were older than the sequoias but died before he could prove it. The forestry people went on with Schulman's work, but did not push it. Then in 1964, a geographer from the University of North Carolina asked Forest Service permission to cut a bristlecone near the Nevada–Arizona border to verify certain Little Ice Age dates. The request was granted almost routinely.

Specialists in dating trees take cores, which leaves the tree unharmed. For his own reasons, the scientist cut down this tree, identified only by number, WPN–114. His report gives statistics: circumference, 252 inches; one dead crown 17 feet high, one living shoot 11 feet high; a single 19-inch strip of bark; mean ring-width, 0.47 mm; counted rings, 4,844. In other words, since rings are not absolutes, this bristlecone pine was approximately five thousand years old. And still alive, still growing, until the chain saw put an end to the oldest living thing on Earth, so far as we know at this time.

Pinyon Pine

PINUS EDULIS

The pinyons grow only in the dry, sandy soil of the West and Southwest. They want nothing to do with New England. A friend grew three or four from seed in his greenhouse and gave me one of them to plant in a dry place in our garden. It lived about a month, then died overnight, probably a victim of homesickness. The pinyons of special memory were in Colorado and Nevada.

These trees have no appeal to lumbermen. They are small, seldom as much as forty feet tall, and usually misshapen, sometimes resembling Indian squaws with packs on their backs. But they produce edible nuts, nuts big as small peanuts and of special flavor. That is their reason for being, and for my special memories.

One memory is of Nevada, not far from Carson City. I went to the pinyon groves there with Paiute Indian friends, gathered pinyon cones, became smeared with resin, which is thick on the cones as they ripen, and had a wonderful holiday. I took a gunnysackful of pinyon cones back to town and let them lie in the sun a few days till they opened. Squirrels got half the nuts, but I still had a quart of my own.

The other memory is of Mesa Verde, in southwestern Colorado. I have known Mesa Verde since the 1920s, but until my wife and I stopped there in the fall of 1965 I had never been there in pinyon-nut time. By sheer chance we hit it right, to the day, the hour. We drove along a remote trail and came to a place where the pinyon nuts had fallen like hail that day. They were in windrows at the roadside. We stopped, and we pushed the squirrels aside long enough to gather two quarts of those wonderful nuts in a paper bag and felt rich as Montezuma.

Red Pine

PINUS RESINOSA

This northeastern pine is sometimes called Norway pine, although it is as native American as corn. It is a darker green tree than white pine and the needles come in bundles of two. They are long, four to six inches, and though flexible they break easily when bent double. The tree's trunk is straight and reddish-gray, much lighter in color than white pine. In Maine the red pine sometimes reaches a height of one hundred feet and is an important timber tree. Its cones, which ripen the first year, are only about two-and-a-half inches long and have no barbs or prickles on their scales. They remain on the trees all winter, though the winged seeds all fall the first autumn.

Red pine persists in areas with sandy soil, all through northern New England, in northern Connecticut, and west as far as Wisconsin and northeastern Minnesota. It is fairly common in the mountains of southern New Hampshire. It is an important timber tree, with a tall, straight central stem that reaches a diameter of two to three feet.

The bark forms irregular diamond-shaped plates. The wood is close-grained, hard, and strong. Its sapwood is almost white, though the dominant color of red pine lumber is pale tan-yellow. Now it is most used for framing, for piles, masts, spars, and other ship fittings. It is heavier than white pine, thirty pounds per square foot compared to twenty-four. I am sure some of the old houses here in my corner of Connecticut have red pine floors. It is one of the most durable of all the pine woods available in this area. The old records say red pine bark was used occasionally for tanning leather.

Tamarack

L A R I X   L A R I C I N A

The tamarack, or hackmatack as some call it, and its relatives are our only deciduous conifers. It sheds all its needles every autumn. The needles are only about an inch long. In spring they are bright golden-yellow-green, in summer a warm blue-green, darker than the pines, and rich golden tan in the autumn. In spring, just before the new needles appear, the tamaracks are aglow with blossoms, the male flowers golden yellow, the females bright red with green tips, all of them very small. The female flowers mature into tiny cones, no more than three-quarters of an inch long, which stay on the tree all winter, shedding seeds.

Tamarack grows very tall and slender, sometimes as much as ninety feet high with a trunk diameter of two feet at most. The western larch, a close relative, sometimes grows to a height of two hundred feet or more with a trunk diameter of only three to four feet. The tree is of slow growth, taking about two hundred and fifty years to reach a trunk diameter of twenty inches.

Tamaracks prefer damp soil and often grow at the edges of swamps, but in my area they can sometimes be found well up on the hillsides. They are essentially a northern tree, growing farther north than any other American species. Even here in New England they prefer the north slopes, the cooler places.

Tamarack wood is heavy and durable, has been used for railroad ties, telephone poles, and fenceposts. The Indians used tamarack rootlets to sew birch bark together in making canoes. They probably also told old John Josselyn, the first naturalist in the Bay Colony, something of the tree's medical virtues. Josselyn wrote: "The Turpentine that issueth from the Larch Tree is singularly good to heal wounds and to draw out malice of any Ache by rubbing the place therewith."

Black Spruce

PICEA MARIANA

Three native spruces grow in my area, the black, the red, and the white, but not many of any of them. Black spruce, also called bog spruce, is the easiest to find. Black spruce and white spruce look much alike—tall, handsome trees with many short bluish-green needles. The red spruce is a smaller tree but otherwise much the same. White spruce is also called skunk spruce because the needles have a definitely skunky odor when they're bruised.

Spruces are sometimes mistaken for balsam firs, which often are planted in our area for Christmas trees. The firs, however, have needles that persistently curve upward, and the spruce needles have no curl to them; they grow all around the twigs, on every side, like the hair on the tail of an angry cat. And the cones on the two species are absolute identification marks. Those on the fir sit up on the branch, while those on the spruce dangle. Both species are grown and cut for Christmas trees, but the firs are better because they hold their needles longer and have a more pleasant odor.

Spruce wood varies with the species. That of the slow-growing red spruce is fine-grained and in demand for sounding boards on pianos. The coarser black and white spruce are sometimes sawed into lumber for sheathing, clapboard, and flooring. Any grade of spruce is used for wood pulp in paper mills. Whole forests of Canadian spruce, most of it black spruce, which grows quickly, are cut every year to make the paper that is fed through the newspaper presses every day.

Spruce beer is made from a decoction of fresh twigs and needles of either the red spruce or the black spruce.

Norway Spruce

P I C E A   A B I E S

A hundred years or so ago someone must have come through this area with a cartload of spruce seedlings and sold or bartered them to the farm folk and townsmen. I can think of no other reason for so many big Norway spruces hereabout, most of them evidently the same age. There is one here in our dooryard, so close to the house I can reach out my study window and touch one of its branches. It is a beautiful tree. By my calculation, after triangulating it, this tree is close to a hundred feet tall. At breast height it is two feet through. Two-thirds of the way to the top it shows, if you look closely, that the top was broken out, long ago, and one of the upper limbs took its place, leading the way upward. Now the tree looks symmetrical and unharmed, from a little distance.

We call it a Norway spruce, as do the owners of all the others of its kind. But it shows many of the characteristics of the tiger-tail spruce, *Picea polita*, a closely related tree native to the Orient and also widely planted in Europe and North America. Its limbs curve downward, then up, and its twigs hang pendulously. The needles curve upward. But the cones are larger than those of the typical tiger-tail, five to seven inches, and the scales are not notched. Perhaps it is a hybrid.

Whatever it is, it is a noble tree. In the spring it sheds pollen literally by the cupful—I have swept up almost a pint of that powdery yellow dust from our front porch. It bears a big crop of cones. The squirrels love it. So do we.

Eastern Hemlock

TSUGA CANADENSIS

There are ten species of hemlock, four of them native to North America. Others grow in Japan, Taiwan, China, and the Himalayas. The botanical name, *Tsuga*, comes from the Japanese word for the larch tree, the tamarack. But let's not get snarled up in names at this point. What we are talking about is the hemlock, and if the Japanese want to call it a larch, and if the botanists go along, that is their problem.

We have a good many hemlocks on our mountainside, and they are beautiful trees. They are known to prefer high ground, and they certainly do here, growing all the way to the summits. Their drooping limbs form splendid shelters for deer. I have taken refuge under a big hemlock in a heavy snowstorm and been warm and dry until I tried to make my way out and get home. Then I always managed to nudge one of those long, sweeping branches and set off a snowslide down that whole side of the tree, right down the neck of my coat.

Hemlocks also thrive in the Adirondacks. In Vermont and Massachusetts they are common in deep woods; they are locally common in Connecticut; and they are common in cold swamps and rocky woods west to Minnesota and south down the mountains to Georgia and Alabama. As a timber tree the hemlock seldom grows over seventy-five or eighty feet tall or five feet in diameter. Its lumber is fairly light in weight, tough, coarse-grained, tends to splinter, and is durable underground. It is used primarily for framing, in carpentry.

The inner bark of hemlock is rich in tannic acid and was long used in leather-making. A suffusion of the bark was used by the Indians as an astringent and a linament for rheumatism. A poultice of hemlock needles and flax seed was used for swellings. The powdered bark contains narcotic properties.

Eastern Redcedar

JUNIPERUS VIRGINIANA

We call it pasture cedar, because it creeps down from the woodland into our pastures and because the birds plant it in their droppings along our pasture fences. One cross-fence in our lower pasture has a row of young cedars almost a hundred yards long, and every fence on this place has at least a few cedars marking the line, some of them fifteen or twenty feet tall. Up in the woods they grow in clusters around older, parent trees; when we need fenceposts we can go up there and cut them—there's no need to go wandering all over the mountainside.

These cedars are rather handsome trees, from a little distance. Up close they often have a scraggled, rusty look. If there is a white pine nearby the contrast is severe—the pine is green, neat, shapely; the cedar is shabby, looks half-dead, and is misshapen. The hungry deer have torn off branch tips in February's starvation nights. In spring, when they grow new foliage at the tips of the twigs, there are points and prickles almost as sharp as raspberry thorns.

Still, I admire these cedars. They like the soil in my area, which is full of limestone. They fill the gaps in the woodland, help check erosion. They make durable fenceposts. A friend of mine who owns a hillside house near the lake just the other side of our mountain has let the cedars grow and now has a splendid grove that he prefers to pines. The cedars, he says, are cleaner and quieter.

The Indians of the West used a decoction of redcedar fruit and twigs for coughs. It is said that redcedar tea and decoction, used as a drink and as a bath, cured Asiatic cholera among the Teton Dakotas in 1849–50.

Barberry

B E R B E R I S   S P P .

There are three more or less common barberries in my area, the American, the European, and the Japanese. The European barberry, *Berberis vulgaris*, is subject to and a host for wheat rust, a fungus disease, and is banished from wheat-growing areas. The Japanese species, *Berberis thurnbergii*, is immune to the rust; it is more or less commonly grown in hedges and is frequently found growing wild in old pastures and fencerows, where it has been planted by bird droppings.

The native American barberry, *Berberis canadensis*, is viciously armed with long thorns that often are branched and even clustered, yet when it comes to bloom in the spring it always disarms me. Until then I am ready to grub it out, wherever it is. But once I see those beautiful golden-yellow blossoms, I think of the crop of scarlet berries it will have in September—and I welcome it.

The European barberry is, to me, a dull, uninteresting plant, fit only for hostile hedges to keep prowlers at bay. The Japanese barberry has greenish-white, inconspicuous blossoms and a profusion of dark red, somewhat acid berries that often are preserved or made into jam.

We have several bushes of the Japanese species, long established here. One big bush at the end of the front porch is reserved for brown thrashers. They have been nesting in it for at least ten years, and they are so insistent on exclusive ownership that even my wife and I must avoid that end of the porch during their nesting time. We also have several of the native American species, one on our riverbank, others in the fencerows.

Tuliptree

L I R I O D E N D R O N   T U L I P I F E R A

This tree is also called white wood; and in the Appalachian Mountains, where it once was cut extensively for lumber, it is known as yellow poplar, though it is quite unrelated to the poplars. It is a big, handsome tree that commonly grows to seventy-five feet in height and, in most favored areas, to a hundred and fifty or a hundred seventy-five feet with a trunk diameter as great as eight feet. The trunk usually is straight and continuous right up to the crown.

The leaves of the tuliptree are readily recognizable, something like maple leaves but squared off at the tip and rounded at the base. But it is the blossoms that make the tuliptree unmistakable. Those blossoms are big, as much as four inches across, and shaped like tulips. They are pale yellowish-green in color with a strong orange band at the base. There are six obovate petals and many long, slim pale green anthers. The trees bloom in May and June. The fruit is a conspicuous, conelike packet of winged seeds that is borne erect on the twigs.

The tuliptree's northern range includes central and western Massachusetts, southern Michigan, and Illinois, and it extends southward all the way to the Gulf except in Florida, where it is scarce. We have a few, a very few, tuliptrees in my corner of Connecticut.

The tree's wood is white, easily worked, and very light in weight. Indians used it for dugout canoes, and Daniel Boone is said to have made a canoe sixty feet long from a tuliptree log. For years it provided most of the lumber sawed in North Carolina. It was used for many of the same purposes as white pine. Today most of the big trees have been cut and the small ones go to the mills for paper pulp.

Sassafras

Once you see and know a sassafras tree, you will never fail to recognize another. Those leaves are unmistakable. They come in several shapes, all on the same tree. There is the plain elliptical, rather blunt-tipped leaf. There is the double-lobed leaf, with a kind of thumb on each side. And there are the two single-lobed leaves that look something like a mitten, sometimes for the right hand, sometimes for the left. The leaves are deep, lustrous green above, somewhat paler beneath.

The blossoms are small, greenish-yellow, and they appear in April or whenever the leaves burst bud and begin to grow. They develop into small, ovoid berrylike fruits, deep blue in color and borne on thick red stems. But the fruit is of no consequence. The tree has long been renowned for its essence, the fragrant sap and juice in its leaf, its bark, and especially its roots.

Nicholás Monardes, a Spanish physician, after a trip to the West Indies and Florida in 1574, announced that sassafras was a cure for almost every human ailment. From then on for more than a century sassafras was a major treasure sought by explorers of this New World. As late as 1610, sassafras was exported to England by Captain John Smith from Jamestown. But eventually its reputation waned and it was considered only a tonic, not a panacea, one of the few tonics that tasted good. And from that rank it became a common backcountry tea that "purifies the blood," its status today.

But in autumn it is a beautiful tree, yellow, orange, bright red, sometimes pink, unforgettable in any woodland.

Sycamore

PLATANUS OCCIDENTALIS

The sycamore has a number of other names: planetree, buttonwood, buttonball-tree, white wood, water beech, virginia maple. Its leaves are shaped somewhat like those of a maple, but no one would mistake this tree for a maple if its trunk and bark were visible. The bark is smooth and pied or patterned, white in big patches, light gray in others, and pale tan and greenish elsewhere. This is because the outer bark keeps peeling off, not in strips but in irregularly shaped patches, and the layer under that outer bark looks so white at first that it appears to be frost-covered.

The sycamore is the biggest deciduous tree in North America. Examples with a trunk diameter of forty-five feet have been found—and long since cut down, unhappily—and at its most luxuriant the tree has been known to grow more than two hundred feet tall. Hollow sycamores in the Midwest—and many of the big ones were hollow—were often used by early pioneers as barns and even as temporary houses for their families. But many pioneers shied away from areas where the sycamores grew because they were low, damp, and tended to be malarial, though the people of that day were as likely to blame malaria on the trees as on the atmosphere and the mosquitoes.

The wood of the sycamore has been used for a great variety of purposes. Slices of a sound sycamore log made good cartwheels. Lengths of hollow sycamore logs, with bottoms nailed on, made serviceable barrels. Slats, paneling, furniture, railroad cars, all were once made of sycamore. Now it is seldom cut for any purpose. Besides, all the giants among the sycamores were cut years ago.

Sweetgum

L I Q U I D A M B A R   S T Y R A C I F L U A

Winter botanizing, especially trying to identify deciduous trees without leaves to guide the way, can try one's patience. Sometimes you can place a tree in its proper family by the shape of its naked silhouette, or the look of the bark. So, you're pretty sure you've got an oak, but which oak? The hickory by the fenceline has shaggy bark, but that's not conclusive proof it's a shagbark hickory. At this point, if you're persistent, you get out a magnifying lens and begin examining buds, leaf scars, twigs, the pith, while referring to complex keys.

A few trees, however, continue to shout their names long after the foliage has fallen—the sweetgum, for instance. Though empty of seeds, its unique fruits hang from the branchlets all winter long, hard spiny balls an inch and a half in diameter. The sweetgum's leaves also are remarkable—star-shaped, up to seven inches long, thick and leathery with deeply cut lobes. And they depart in a blaze of glory. In a nearly pure stand of sweetgums, the autumn color of those five-pointed stars can land any place on the spectrum between orange and fire-engine red.

A kin of witch-hazel, sweetgum belongs to a minuscule genus of only four or five species of trees, the others found in Asia. *Liquidambar* means, literally, "liquid amber" and refers to the pleasant-tasting resin that the tree exudes when you peel away the deeply furrowed bark. Pioneers used it for chewing gum and homemade medicines. Early in this century it was used commercially for making soaps, adhesives, and drugs. And the dark, reddish-brown wood is valued as a veneer for fine furniture. In some areas, sweetgum is second only to oak in hardwood production.

Sweetgum is largely a tree of the southeastern states, although its range stretches northward along the Atlantic coast into Connecticut. On rich alluvial soils, sweetgum can attain a height of a hundred and thirty feet, usually growing in association with tuliptrees, hickories, oaks, and bald-cypresses. In many southern towns, it is as widely planted for shade as maples are in northern communities.

L . L .

Witch-Hazel

HAMAMELIS VIRGINIANA

Anyone seeing witch-hazel in bloom for the first time could be excused for exclaiming: "This is mad!" Witch-hazel blooms in October, and its blossoms look like a tangle of long, narrow, bright yellow ribbons. There are only four petals, but they twist and curl so much they make a veritable tousle. And in October! And when the flowers appear, last year's seed capsules mature, fat little round pods with flaring lips. When ripe, those pods split down the middle with explosive force and fling their seeds, four to a pod, as much as twenty-five or thirty feet. Thus does the witch-hazel distribute its seedlings and create thickets of its own kind.

Among the Oneida Indians of upper New York state, the witch-hazel was called *Oe-eh-nah-kwe-ha-he*, a laughing kind of name that is said to mean spotted stick. The shrub's medicinal qualities are said to have been discovered by one of the Oneidas. Witch-hazel extract is obtained by distilling the shrub's bark and twigs. In some areas of New England I have seen witch-hazel brush cut and piled in windrows, ready to be hauled to the regional plant where it was steamed and the extract distilled for market.

Witch-hazel usually grows as a shrub about ten to twelve feet high, but now and then it becomes a scraggly tree as tall as twenty-five feet. We had such a tree in our backyard near Stamford, Connecticut, which probably was the last one of a witch-hazel clump that once covered that hillside. Nobody in his right mind would have planted a witch-hazel there, in the middle of an old chicken run. But the last I knew, it was still there, though the chickens and their run were long gone; it was a small but sturdy tree, stubbornly blooming every October.

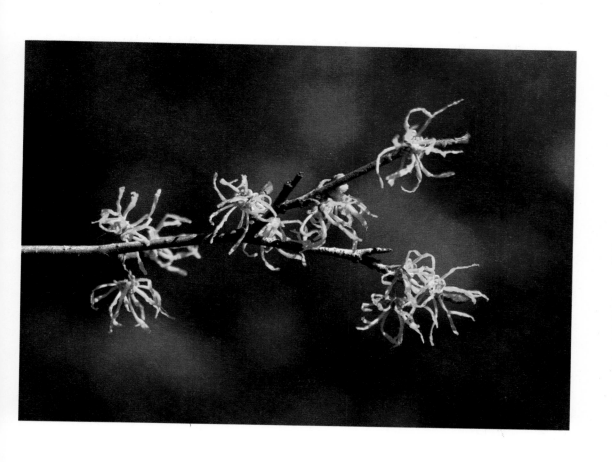

American Elm

ULMUS AMERICANA

This tree is also called white elm or soft elm. It grows virtually all over this country east of the Rockies. Many towns in Ohio, Indiana, and Iowa have their village greens and their big elms—or did have until the elm blight struck—that could be moved right into New England and be entirely at home. The people who first settled there, of course, were primarily New Englanders, and they built their midwestern towns on the New England village model, elm trees and all.

The American elm, despite tradition, is not always the classic vase or fountain shape. Many of the elms are—especially those around New England village greens—but the tree also grows in a heavy, horizontal-limbed shape called the oak form. We have one that branches only five feet from the ground and sweeps outward, not directly up. I have never seen an elm with a central trunk running all the way to its tip.

These elms grow big. I have heard it said by those who should know that one big elm will have a million leaves with a full acre of leaf surface. Many Connecticut elms reach a height of more than one hundred feet and a trunk girth of twenty feet.

The early settlers didn't think much of the elms. The wood was tough, hard to split, but rooted in contact with the soil. As lumber it warped, and it was poor firewood. In either case, it often had the smell of urine, and hence was called piss elm by country folk. But even they admitted that it was a beautiful tree.

Unfortunately, the elms have been in serious trouble since the 1930s when a fungus disease, *Graphium ulmi*, was brought to this country in elm logs imported from England to be peeled for veneer. The elm bark beetle carried the infection and it soon was killing elms by the dozens, then the hundreds, all across the country. No cure for the disease has been found.

Slippery Elm

U L M U S   R U B R A

I was perhaps five years old and we were visiting at my maternal grand-father's farm in eastern Nebraska. This day he and my Uncle Arthur were getting rid of two trees that a windstorm had knocked over in one of the lower pastures. I was allowed to go with them. The trees were slippery elms. I thought that meant one could slide down their trunks as down a greased pole, maybe. Uncle Arthur laughed at me, but Grandfather pulled off a strip of the thick, gray bark and peeled from it a layer of inner bark that was white and greasy-looking. He handed it to me and said, "Chew it. It's good."

I tried to chew it and found it was too tough to bite off, but I got a taste of the sap that made it look greasy. It was a rather sickening sweet flavor, just slightly nauseating. But Grandfather stripped a piece for himself, folded it, and put it into his mouth. I, no less a man at that point, folded my piece, put it into my mouth, and chewed. It didn't taste bad, really. But I didn't ask for seconds.

That was my introduction to slippery elm. I can get it today at the nearest drugstore, if I really want it. It is used in everyday tonics and remedies for various complaints, and I am sure it never harmed anyone.

As a tree, the slippery elm is not even in the same class with the Ameri-can elm. It is relatively small, fifty or sixty feet high, but with a sturdy trunk. Its lumber is of no commercial value. Its leaves are big, two to three inches wide, five to seven inches long. Its seeds have broad, circular tissue-wings, bigger than those of the American elm.

Hackberry

CELTIS OCCIDENTALIS

The first year we came to this farm I noticed the young elms in the fence-row along our lower pasture. They were nice trees, about twenty-five feet high, and I saw no reason to remove them. I like trees in a fencerow. I like fencerows, which make shelter and food for birds and small animals.

In September, however, I noticed that there was a circle of dark, cherry-like fruit under two of those young elms, a purplish smear on the hardtop road, and a great many small fruit pits. I took a closer look then, and found that those two trees were not elms, though their leaves looked much like elm leaves at a casual glance. Their warty, corky bark told me they were hack-berries. And when I began watching for them, I found a surprising number of hackberry trees along other fences, where they undoubtedly passed as young elms.

Now, twenty-odd years later, I am doubly grateful for those hack-berries. There they stand, ripening their sweet little berries every autumn—another common name for them is sugarberry, by the way—while most of the young elms that were in that fencerow have been blighted and cut down and burned. The blight obviously does not attack hackberries.

The hackberry grows from eastern Massachusetts to northwestern Ne-braska and from the St. Lawrence River to Florida. It has no particular use as lumber, though the trees sometimes grow fifty or sixty feet high. It is used for cheap furniture, for barrel staves, for boxes and crates. But birds like the tree, and 'possums do. And I do, too.

Sweetfern

C O M P T O N I A   P E R E G R I N A

"Can you tell me," the voice on the telephone asked, "which fern book I should look in to find sweetfern? I have looked and looked, and I can't find it anywhere."

I had to tell the woman to put away her fern books and look in a handbook on shrubs. Sweetfern, I told her, is a first cousin of the bayberry.

"Well, what were the botanists doing when they called it sweetfern?" she demanded.

"It wasn't the botanists," I said. "It was the country folk, like you and me, who called it sweetfern. I am sure my grandmother gathered it to put with her linens. I remember her speaking of 'that sweet fern smell,' and my thinking that all ferns smelled that way."

Reluctantly the woman at the other end of the telephone line accepted it. She would look in her shrub book.

Sweetfern grows only about two feet tall. Its woody stems are dull red or brown, and its leaves are long and narrow, with many small, rounded lobes, so they look somewhat like a fern frond. They are dark green above, very pale green below. Their fruit comes in a small, bristly, spherical bur. This bur and the leaves are strongly aromatic when crushed. The leaves, as I told the woman who inquired, were often used to scent linens in Colonial days and still are so used by some rural housewives. They are simply plucked and put in the linen drawers or between the sheets and towels stored there.

Black Walnut

J U G L A N S   N I G R A

When it was reported that thieves had stolen the trunk of a black walnut tree from a cow pasture not fifty miles from here, it seemed incredible. But a little figuring showed why they took that tree and left the cows untouched. Peeled for surfacing on fancy plywood, that black walnut log would be worth more than fifteen thousand dollars.

Black walnut trees are rare in my corner of the country. In one little area near where I live they once grew as readily as willows, but elsewhere in New England the butternuts and the hickories dominated. Most of the walnuts around here were cut for gunstocks in the two World Wars. Those now left are mostly stragglers and cripples.

The black walnut is not really beautiful. It has a sturdy central stalk or trunk, but it tends to be a broad tree, without grace. Its leaves are long and have fifteen or more leaflets opposite each other. Its fruits are black, rough-coated nuts enclosed in thick, yellowish-green husks rich in a very dark brown dye. The meat of the nuts is rich, oily, and distinctly flavored. The outer hulls were used by pioneers as dyestuff for wool used to knit stockings. Anyone who picks or hulls walnuts has dark-dyed hands that do not bleach back to normal color for weeks.

Squirrels gather and hoard black walnuts. They know more about nuts than we do. Some years ago a man who wanted walnut seedlings planted a hundred nuts in a row four inches deep. A few days later he found that squirrels had dug up ninety-two of those nuts. The other eight were right where they had been planted. The man dug them up, cracked them open, and found that none had a live kernel in it. The squirrels apparently knew that without even digging them up.

Butternut

J U G L A N S   C I N E R E A

The butternut is New England's black walnut. It grows in the Midwest, too, out as far as Nebraska; but it is traditional in New England. As a tree, it is smaller than the black walnut, more branched, and more scraggly. Its leaves are compound, just like those of the black walnut, but they have longer stems and fewer leaflets, so the trees look sparsely leafed.

The nuts of the butternut are long and oval, but otherwise much like those of the black walnut, with that outer green husk, the black inner hull deeply corrugated, the sweet nutmeat sectioned in this tough, hard-to-crack hull. The shell or husk of the butternut has bristly little hairs that are full of a dark brown dye, but the inside of that husk has a yellowish-orange dye.

The meat of the butternut is flavored much like that of the black walnut, but it is more oily and it tends to go rancid. Indians and pioneers made oil from the butternuts and used it on their hair. Not many people seem to know now, but butternut sap makes good sugar, just like maple sap. It takes about four times as much sap from the butternut tree, however, as it does from a sugar maple to make a quart of syrup.

Butternut wood is relatively light in weight and easily worked. It is soft-textured and has a satiny finish. It was used in building fine carriages and is still used for interior finish in houses, where it does not warp or crack and seems to mellow with age. Many fine old American church altars were made of carved butternut wood.

Pecan

C A R Y A   I L L I N O E N S I S

The pecan is not native to my area. The closest it comes is Ohio. But it gets space here because it is an especially good nut tree—both Jefferson and Washington planted and grew magnificent pecan trees in Virginia—and because it illustrates a pioneer stupidity about natural resources that is almost incredible.

Pecan belongs to the hickory family. In Texas, one state to which it is native, it grows to tremendous size, sometimes a hundred and twenty feet high with a trunk thirty feet around. Its enormous limbs may spread its crown to a diameter of a hundred feet. The thin-shelled nuts, in their oval green husks, are one of the major nut crops of America. Well before settlers crossed the Alleghenies, traders and trappers brought pecan nuts to the coastal settlements, and plantation owners planted them. Thus grew many pecan groves from Virginia southward.

For many years only wild pecans came to market. The method of harvesting those wild ones now seems unbelievable. Nut-gatherers went through the woods, chose the largest, heaviest-bearing pecan trees, and when the nuts were ripe they cut down the trees. Then they put boys to work picking the nuts from the fallen giants. And that was the end of those pecan trees, forever. Next year they cut more trees to gather the nuts. Not until those magnificent pecan trees became scarce did they cease cutting them and begin planting and grafting new trees to replace the ones so stupidly destroyed. Today pecan trees are planted and grown in orchards like oranges.

Unlike most other members of the walnut family, the pecan is not particularly valued for its lumber. The nuts are its primary asset.

Shagbark Hickory

CARYA OVATA

The shagbark, or shellbark as it is sometimes called, is the classic American hickory, probably the toughest tree on the continent. Weight for weight, our hickory is stronger than steel, more elastic, and less heat-conductive. As fuel, it outranks coal, with more heat in it, pound for pound, than anthracite. Besides, the shagbarks have some of the sweetest nuts that grow in the woodland.

What more can you ask of a tree?

The shagbark gets its name honestly. A mature tree has smoke-gray bark that is forever separating into large plates, sometimes six inches wide and a foot and a half long, that curl away from the trunk at both ends. This gives a shaggy look to the tree, visible as far as you can see the tree itself, shaggy as a bear. This shagginess may start in fairly young trees, and at the base of old hickories there may be a whole pile of these bark plates, torn loose by the weather.

I marvel at the way a shagbark, or any hickory for that matter, opens its buds in the spring. Those big terminal buds are fat as a man's thumb. Their time approaches and they begin to twist, half open though with their tips still closed. Finally they twist themselves loose, and the whole bud and its contents are in sight, a yellow-green sheath tinged with red, and emerging from it the whole cluster of new leaves, tightly curled, and the catkins inside the leaves. It is like a miracle. No human hands ever packed half so much into so small a space.

Pioneers made boxes of hickory bark. They made ramrods for their guns from hickory wood; they made rungs for their chairs from it. They also made hoops for their barrels from hickory, hinges for their cabin doors, and handles for their axes.

Pignut Hickory

CARYA GLABRA

This tree is also called black hickory or broom hickory. It has much smoother bark than shagbark hickory, though at a certain age some pignut hickories show platelike scales smaller than those of the shagbark. But lumbermen make no distinction between the two trees. Its wood is used for tool handles, for skis, for anything that must sustain violent strains or twists. It formerly was used for making the hubs of wagon wheels, and even for the felloes of those wheels. It was, and still is, used in making American racing sulkies. And its smaller limbs were used for pioneer brooms, whittled down into strips that were folded down over the butt of the stick, tied there, and the handle carved to size. This made a stiff, very effective broom for cabin floors.

Unlike the shagbark hickory, the pignut has nuts that are not worth gathering. They are small, whitish-yellow when the outer shell opens, and have nutmeat that is insipid or bitter. When swine were let run in the woods, the pigs ate these nuts and apparently relished them—hence the name. The shagbark nut is enclosed in a round green husk. That of the pignut is in a pear-shaped husk.

The leaves of the two trees are much alike, compound with five leaflets to a stem, sometimes seven—always seven on the shellbark. In autumn the leaves turn a bright golden yellow before they begin to "rust" with patches of brown. Their bright color does not last more than a few days. Then the leaves come down in a thick shower and the trees stand in winter nakedness.

Hazelnut

C O R Y L U S   A M E R I C A N A

Hazelnut, also called filbert, is a shrub sometimes eight feet high, common in fencerows and thickety growth at the edge of timber patches. Its leaves are narrowly pointed or heart-shaped, rough above, pale below, three to five inches long. The staminate catkins are three to four inches long and bloom in April, when the early bees welcome them and spend long hours gathering their pollen. The fruit is a small, chestnut-brown nut, almost perfectly spherical, enclosed in a pair of broad, leafy, toothed bracts with many bristles at the base. The nutmeat is sweet and furnishes most of the hazelnuts on the market. They ripen in September.

A similar shrub, the beaked hazelnut, *Corylus rostrata*, grows in hedgerows and thickets over much of the same area as the above species and also farther north. In virtually all details the two shrubs are the same, but the beaked hazelnuts are enclosed in a husk that terminates in a long, tubular beak. This hazelnut grows all across the continent, to the Pacific slope.

We have a number of hazelnut bushes in our fencerows, and for years I planned to gather enough nuts to have occasional winter evenings of nut feasts, with hazelnuts, hickory nuts, and butternuts or black walnuts. But never yet have I been able to gather more than a scant handful of hazelnuts. The squirrels always beat me to them. I have tried picking them early, but they have no substance then. I have tried covering them with cheesecloth, but the squirrels go right through or under. Now I know I shall have to admire the bushes, envy the squirrels, and buy my hazelnuts at the market.

American Beech

FAGUS GRANDIFOLIA

We haven't as many beech trees in my area as I would wish, but the species is native to the whole eastern half of the country north of Florida. Beeches are particularly handsome trees with their big, smooth boles, smoky-gray bark, wide-spreading branches, and almost luminous leaves. Under the best conditions they grow a hundred feet tall and have a widely rounded crown. At the base of the sturdy trunk, a beech tends to reach out with big, half-exposed roots for a shallow roothold.

It is the bark and the leaves that identify a beech for me at first sight. The bark almost glows, is at times purplish-gray, and invites carved initials. Even on old trees it seldom is rough. It was on a big beech in Washington County, Tennessee, that Daniel Boone carved his memorandum: "D Boone cilled a bar on tree in year 1760." That tree, incidentally, survived until 1916 and was estimated to be three hundred and sixty-five years old, which gives an index to the longevity of the species.

The leaves are elliptical, short-stemmed, and prominently veined. Each vein ends in a marginal tooth. But it is the texture of the leaves that makes them unique. They are almost translucent. In summer the sun shines through them, but not the heat. In early autumn they turn a clean, soft yellow. As autumn advances, some but by no means all the beech leaves fall. Those that remain turn almost white—phantom leaves, soft as facial tissue—and cling there through the winter.

The beechnuts, something like miniature chestnuts, are borne in a bur with weak spines. Passenger pigeons once lived on them. Later, the pioneer's hogs ate them. Today some country folk gather and savor them. The tree's wood is considered inferior for lumber. But I still insist that it is one of the most beautiful trees in the woodland.

American Chestnut

CASTANEA DENTATA

Most people speak of the American chestnut in the past tense, and perhaps they are right. It may be gone forever, victim of the chestnut blight that apparently came from abroad and attacked native trees in New York City's zoological park in 1904. From there it spread with astonishing speed, across New Jersey, into Pennsylvania, and north and east into and through New England, then into the Midwest. The blight is a spore disease, and the spores are windborne. The fungus enters the tree through any crack or hole in the outer bark and destroys the cambium layer, the tree's circulatory system. The tree dies, but the fungus lives on, producing more spores to kill other trees.

There once were great chestnut forests in the East and the Midwest. Now they are gone, cut either when first blighted or when the blight attacked their area. We still have old stumps in our area, and sprouts grow from those stumps, sometimes to a diameter of three inches. But they seldom bloom and almost never produce nuts. A friend from upper New York state coddled such sprouts on his own farm, got a handful of fertile nuts from one of them, and grew seedlings from the nuts. He gave me one of those seedlings, which grew into a tree four inches through and fifteen feet high. Then the blight struck it and now all I have is a clump of sprouts from its root.

Such sprouts grow on our New England hillsides, tantalizing in their reminder of a better day. Possibly an immune strain may someday appear. Meanwhile, the only immune chestnuts we know are of the Chinese strain, though a scattered few American chestnuts are known to be surviving in remote places.

White Oak

QUERCUS ALBA

The oak is commonly considered to be the toughest, most durable of all our common forest trees. It isn't, really, but in overall quality it comes in either at or close to the top. The British in Colonial days scorned American oak for their ships, but we built our own ships of our own oak and proved that they were equal to or better than the British ones. And on land we have used oak, primarily white oak, for stout timbers in blockhouses, mills, bridges, barns, log cabins, and other structures. It has been the best all-round hardwood in America. White pine warps less, hickory is more resilient, locust is more durable. But our white oak stands second in each category.

This tree grows to tremendous size, with a spread of more than a hundred and twenty-five feet, a trunk twenty-five or more feet in circumference, and a height of ninety to a hundred feet. It also grows as a bush at altitudes of four thousand feet or more in the southern Appalachians. It is a beautiful tree. When its leaves first burst from the bud in the spring they clothe the white oak with a mist of red that slowly turns to pink before the true green of the leaves. In the autumn the foliage turns a rich red, the color of Burgundy wine, then fades to various shades of brown. And the leaves tend to cling to the branches all winter.

The white oak's acorns, maturing the first year, are choice food for squirrels and birds. When they fall and come into contact with the soil they soon germinate and thrust roots into the ground before hard frost. Those acorns can be eaten raw, like chestnuts, but they are sweeter if they are boiled or roasted first.

White oak has been used for roofing, for flooring, and for tight barrels. America went through the "golden oak" era in furniture, which produced some amazingly ugly tables, chairs, and chests. It also at one time was used for interior paneling, with no great success in an esthetic sense. But it still is good durable wood, with its own type of beauty.

Post Oak

QUERCUS STELLATA

This oak got its common name from the pioneers who, having found that it was durable in contact with the soil, used it for fenceposts. It also was used for cross-ties on the early railroads. It makes poor lumber because it is a knotty tree, so it was seldom used in building; and it is too tough for use in paper pulp. For these reasons the post oak has persisted in sizeable stands in the mountains and along the coastal plains. Much of the oak in the Ozarks is post oak.

The post oak grows from southern New England all the way to Florida and west to and in places beyond the Mississippi. It grows in Texas, for example, and as I mentioned, in the Ozarks of Arkansas. Here in Connecticut it is found in coastal areas from New Haven southward, and inland we have scattered growths of it, particularly here in the western hills.

The tree's bark is a warm reddish-brown with broad ridges. Except in the South, it seldom grows more than fifty feet high and it branches freely, making a somewhat tangled crown. The leaves are four to six inches long, with their biggest lobes near the tip, rounded lobes typical of the white oak. When those leaves first come from the buds in spring they are deep red. They mature into a dark green summer color. In autumn they turn yellow or yellowish-brown, and many of them persist on the trees all winter, until they are pushed off in the spring by new growth. The acorns, about three-quarters of an inch long, are often striped green and brown, and the cup covers about one-third of the nut. They are sweet enough to be edible.

Blue Oak

QUERCUS DOUGLASII

In spring, the gently rolling hillsides of coastal California are a joy to behold. Rejuvenated by winter's rains, the grasslands turn a blinding green that is broken by waves of golden-orange poppies and the royal-blue spikes of lupines. But by September, they have been baked sere by summer's sun, and the only relief from brown pasture and cloudless sky is provided by weathered oaks that stand sentinel on the hillops or offer an instant of shade in the hot valleys.

California is justly famous for its oaks. The first Franciscan missions were built in oak-wooded valleys, where Indians, for centuries, annually gathred acorns as a food staple. Settlers from the forested East naturally sought out the oaklands for their homes and communities, and more than a hundred and fifty California cities and towns bear such names as Charter Oak, Oak Knolls, Thousand Oaks, Live Oak, Paso Robles.

Fifteen species of oaks are native to California, but four share prominence in the coastal hills and interior valleys, two of them evergreen, two deciduous: coast live oak (*Quercus agrifolia*), which forms the open park-like groves so often seen in movies; interior live oak (*Q. wislizeni*), its counterpart in drier places; valley oak (*Q. lobata*), a large, lovely tree with wide-spreading limbs; and blue oak, which can be told at a distance by its blue-green foliage.

Quercus douglasii honors David Douglas, the Scottish botanist who explored California and the Pacific Northwest in the early nineteenth century. The young botanist's greatest memorial is the Douglas-fir (*Pseudotsuga menziesii* of coastal rain forests, one of the world's tallest trees and our most important source of lumber and plywood. The blue oak—short and stout, often leaning away from Pacific winds—is hardly so magnificent or valuable. Forty-niners shored up their gold mines with blue oak timbers, although the wood turns black when exposed to air and falls victim to dry rot. But wild animals and livestock relish the acorns, and it is a ruggedly picturesque tree. These hills would be incomplete without it.

L . L .

Swamp White Oak

QUERCUS BICOLOR

The swamp white oak seldom grows more than fifty or sixty feet high in my area, but elsewhere, particularly in the South, it reaches twice that height and has a trunk diameter of eight feet. A big tree it is, indeed. And it is a good lumber tree; commercially it is called simply white oak and used for the same purposes as the true white oak. It grows from southern Maine to southern Michigan and western Missouri, and down the Alleghenies to northern Georgia. In New England it is not common, though it is found in Massachusetts, Rhode Island, and Connecticut. It prefers to grow on the borders of streams, ponds, and swamps.

The leaves readily distinguish it from the ordinary white oak. They lack the big lobes we think of as typical of all oak leaves. The swamp white oak's leaves are roughly elliptical, six to eight inches long, with shallowly scalloped lobes on each side, much like rounded teeth. The acorns are deep chestnut red and about one inch long. The cup encloses half the acorn, and the acorns occur in clusters of two or three. They ripen the first year, usually in October, and are edible.

Those big leaves are surprisingly mobile. In any breeze at all they flutter and turn, and you can see a swamp white oak from half a mile away, for it flashes in the sunlight. The undersides of those leaves are silvery, in contrast to the warm green of the upper surfaces. So it gleams and glistens, this oak tree, in every summer breeze. In autumn the leaves turn dull brown, occasionally a rather dull orange, but they have had their summer splendor.

Chinkapin Oak

QUERCUS MUEHLENBERGII

We have two chinkapin oaks, or chinquapins, for both spellings are commonly used. One is a full-fledged tree, the other a shrub that sometimes grows just big enough to be considered a tree. The name comes from *chechinkamin*, which was the Algonquian Indian word for the American chestnut tree and meant "great berry." The Indians naturally prized the delicious, flattened nuts of the doomed chestnut, two or three nuts to each spiny three-inch-wide bur. These oaks are called chinkapins because their leaves resemble those of the chestnut, and possibly also because their own nuts are sweet and edible. Chestnuts and oaks are related, both being members of the beech clan.

Dwarf chinkapin oak (*Quercus prinoides*) is the shrub of the pair, usually growing two to ten feet high with a "trunk" no more than four inches across. But now and then an individual will rise to the occasion and turn into a small tree perhaps eighteen feet tall. Dwarf chinkapin forms thickets on dry, rocky slopes or barren places. It produces an abundant crop of acorns at least once every two years, sometimes each fall. Native to most of the eastern and central states, dwarf chinkapin is easily told by its brushy tendencies and the coarsely toothed leaves that turn rusty red in autumn.

The specific name for chinkapin oak, the tree, honors Henry Ernst Muehlenberg, a botanist in Pennsylvania in the late seventeen and early eighteen hundreds. It is found over much the same area as dwarf chinkapin, but only a few trees at a time; nowhere is it common. Acidic soils on limestone outcrops and dry bluffs are its preferred environment; there it will attain a height of a hundred feet or more.

Chinkapin oak trees, unlike the shrubby chinkapins, drop large crops of acorns three or four years apart. The nuts are an inch long, light brown, covered for half their length by a bowl-shaped cup. Deer, squirrels, raccoons, wild turkeys, and other denizens of the eastern forest feasted on the original chinkapins, those "great berries" of the late great chestnut. The tasty nuts of these two oaks, tree and shrub, make up a small part of the loss.

L . L .

Northern Red Oak

QUERCUS RUBRA

This oak gets its name from the color of its wood, not from its leaves. The heartwood is light brown or reddish-brown, called red by lumbermen. Actually, the leaves are pink when the buds first open, but in the autumn they turn dull brown or a rather bright orange. Those leaves are big, five to eight inches long and four to five inches broad, with deep indentations leaving three or four jagged points on each side and a terminal point as well, pretty much the typical and traditional oak leaf.

This tree is the common oak of New England. It also grows in much of the eastern half of the United States, south to Georgia, west to Nebraska, Kansas, Oklahoma, and western Texas. In the North it grows to seventy-five feet in height, and occasionally more than a hundred feet. Its wood is coarse-grained and porous. In the past it was used for cross-ties for railroads. Nowadays it goes into rough lumber, occasionally into clapboards. It is probably the fastest growing of all the oaks.

It bears large acorns, one to one-and-a-half inches long, in shallow cups. The acorns take two years to ripen and are too bitter to be eaten. The bitterness comes from the tannic acid which makes the oak's bark useful in tanning leather.

It is a handsome tree with a broad, shapely crown, and is often planted along streets and in parks, where it usually grows well.

Pin Oak

QUERCUS PALUSTRIS

The pin oak pleases me for reasons I cannot wholly explain. It is very much the individual, with leaves slimmed down to fundamentals, very deeply cleft, very sharply pointed. Unlike other oaks, it has a central stem that doesn't branch and fork; from this stem grow many slender branches that arch up and out but not far out. Many spurlike branchlets, short and pointed, grow on the main branches. These are called pins and give the tree its common name. In autumn the leaves turn a rich ruby red, making the pin oaks stand out in any growth of trees, especially oaks.

We live at almost the northern limit of its normal range, and we have only a few pin oaks. But forty miles south of here, or fifty miles southwest, this tree is common on the rocky hillsides and even down along the streams. It also grows west, as far as eastern Kansas and northeastern Oklahoma. But it does not grow in the western Alleghenies of Pennsylvania or Virginia.

Pin oak is not a lumberman's wood. Its central trunk would make a good sawlog, but all those small branches make knots, and the result is lumber that is too knotty for most commercial uses. It is a good streetside tree, however, and often is planted in towns in the eastern United States. Even when mature, it takes up little room, is generous with its shade, is not subject to many diseases, roots well and is able to withstand most storms, and makes a gorgeous display in the autumn. All are good reasons, too, to appreciate it when the pin oak grows in a natural woodland. Its acorns, since it belongs to the red oak tribe, are too bitter for us to eat, but are relished by deer, wild turkeys, and especially ducks where the trees grow in the floodplains.

Black Oak

QUERCUS VELUTINA

Some people call this tree dyer's oak, and some call it tanner's oak. Both names indicate old uses for it. The inner bark is yellow or orange, as one can easily see by scratching a twig with a thumbnail. This yellow was used by weavers for years, and is still probably used where the old arts are practiced. And the bark is rich in tannic acid, hence its use by leather tanners. But they had the problem of ridding it of that yellow dye. They usually leached it out.

As lumber, the black oak is rated as just so much second-grade oak, commonly sold as "red oak" and used for framing, for flooring if it can be found relatively knot-free, and for other prosaic purposes. The black oak doesn't lend itself to the lumberman's idea of a good tree. The trunk tends to be short and often crooked, there are many knots, and it cracks, even when still a living tree. It is not a beautiful tree, in form at least, to ingratiate itself with tree-planters. It is thick, heavy in shape, thin at the crown, and scraggly-looking in winter.

Out in the woods, however, it has its own personality—tough, untamed, almost a part of the rocky hillsides and ledgy ridges where it so often grows. And its foliage is russet brown or dull red in autumn. It flowers in May, produces acorns that are light brown in color and approximately one inch long, with a cup that covers about half the nut, which is bitter and inedible.

It grows from southern Maine southward almost to Florida and west into Kansas, Oklahoma, and Texas. Its leaves are typical red oak leaves, with bristled points and about five to six inches long.

Shingle Oak

QUERCUS IMBRICARIA

The tree towering eighty feet over the Ozark River, shading the stream with its broad, rounded crown, was new to me. The rough and furrowed bark and general appearance said "oak," but the leaves were lance-shaped, rather like those of a mountain laurel, not the round-lobed or deeply toothed oak leaves familiar to northerners. We pulled our canoe onto a willow-thick sandbar, then climbed the bank for a closer look.

The oak genus, *Quercus*, is a big one, with some five hundred species of trees and shrubs worldwide, most of them in the Northern Hemisphere. We have fifty-eight native oaks in North America, and almost that many distinctly different shapes of oak leaves. Some are thin and papery, others tough and leathery, even evergreen. The club-shaped leaves of blackjack oak (*Q. marilandica*) explain that scrubby tree's common name. A popular curbside shade tree in the South, the willow oak (*Q. phellos*) has leaves up to five inches long and a mere half-inch wide, suggesting the impossible marriage of an oak with a willow.

If treewatchers kept life-lists like birdwatchers, I would have checked off my first shingle oak. Both the common and scientific names of this handsome tree attest to its former use in shingle-making, *imbricaria* meaning overlapping. Hardly a settler's cabin was built in the lower Ohio River Valley without being finished off with thin slabs of shingle oak wood from the nearest water-powered mill.

Shingle oak thrives in both dry upland and moist riverbank environments. Its acorns are small, about half an inch long. In a good mast year, if you gathered up all the nuts from a mature shingle oak they might fill two bushel baskets. But those acorns are important fuel for wildlife—for turkeys, deer, and squirrels, for quail that pick up pieces of nuts left by squirrels, and especially for mallards and wood ducks that congregate in forested river bottoms across southern Indiana, Illinois, and over in Missouri.

L . L .

American Hornbeam

CARPINUS CAROLINIANA

This large shrub, or small tree, is sometimes called blue beech because its rather smooth, slate-gray bark looks something like the bark of the true beeches. Its leaves look a good deal like birch leaves, two to four inches long. The twigs seem to zigzag, though the hornbeam often forms a shapely shrub.

Male and female flowers appear in early spring, in separate catkins on the same tree. The staminate catkins are long and pendulous, while the short pistillate catkins occur at the very branch-tips. The fruit of the hornbeam is a tiny ribbed nut about one-third of an inch long.

The trunk and larger branches of the hornbeam make the tree easily recognizable, once known. They are loosely spiraled with what look like muscles immediately under the bark—smooth, rounded ridges that make one think of young athletes' arms and legs. This look begins quite early in the tree's growth and continues all its life.

The wood itself is extremely hard and tough. The name comes from *horn* for toughness and *beam*, an old word for tree. In pioneer days the wood sometimes was used for making bowls and dishes because it seldom warped or cracked. The problem was in getting a block of hornbeam big enough to fashion a bowl. It also was used for handles and even for heads of hammers, mallets, and such tools, as well as for levers—but only locally, chiefly by farmers and backwoodsmen. Lumbermen had little use for it; it was too tough for their saws and had little market value.

Sweet Birch

B E T U L A   L E N T A

At first look, this birch can be mistaken for a wild cherry, with its shiny, almost smooth, dark red bark, looking black in some light. The twigs, however, are bright green at first, then turn dark orange-brown, and by the first winter they are a bright brownish-red. The inner bark of the tree and its twigs, at any age, have a strong taste and aroma of wintergreen. The male catkins, three to four inches long, form at the twig tips. Female catkins are less than an inch long, and fat; they form fat packs of seed with scales that stand erect on the twig.

You can't mistake this tree if you taste or smell its twigs. This is because of an essential oil in the tree that is chemically identical with that in the little creeping woodland plant called wintergreen, a cousin of the trailing arbutus. Wintergreen oil, used as a flavoring in drugs and candy, was expensive a century ago, so Appalachian mountaineers, with these sweet birches in their woodlands, began chopping them down, reducing them to chips and extracting the oil with a crude process. Saplings were the best source, but it took about a hundred saplings to produce a quart of oil. So sweet birches were for a time endangered as a species. Then chemists found an easy way to produce synthetic wintergreen oil from wood alcohol and salicylic acid, and the trees were spared. Birch beer is also made from sweet birch, but from the sap, which can be tapped.

Sweet birch once was used in furniture-making, and because it deepened in color with exposure to the air it was sometimes passed off as mahogany. At one time, in fact, it was commercially called mountain mahogany. It is stronger than mahogany and as hard as black cherry.

Yellow Birch

BETULA ALLEGHANIENSIS

This tree is also sometimes called the silver birch. It is the biggest of all the birches, occasionally reaching a height of one hundred feet with a trunk diameter as large as four feet. Early-day stories had it even bigger, up in the North Woods, where it was something of a hearsay tree until 1803, when Andre Michaux, the French botanist who did most of his work here in America, described and named it. But examples of the yellow birch that are bigger than any other tree except the white pine can be found in Canada today.

It has the usual birch characteristics, leaves and catkins and conelike fruit. But its bark is not conspicuous; it is yellowish-bronze, almost brown at times. That bark, however, is a godsend to wilderness travelers wherever the yellow birch grows. Strips of it peel off readily, and it will take fire and burn even when it is wet; you can start a campfire with it in a downpour, as long as you can get a match lit.

In the North the yellow birch grows on cool uplands. In the mid-Atlantic states it finds the coolness it demands only in swampy ground. In the southern Appalachians it is restricted to steep mountainsides, up where the air is cool. It is usually inconspicuous, blending with all the other trees of the woodland. Until autumn, that is. Then its leaves turn a clean, clear golden color. They are unmistakable.

Yellow birch is the most valuable timber tree of all the birches, once used for ox yokes, sledge frames, and wagon-wheel hubs, today used as lumber for interior finish in houses.

River Birch

BETULA NIGRA

Red birch, cinnamon birch, and black birch also are names by which this tree is known, but river birch seems the best choice. For it thrives in wet places—on riverbanks and floodplains, in swamps, and beside lakes and ponds. River birch occurs sporadically in southern New England—I have two or three mature trees in my creekside patch of woods, plus uncountable saplings—but the species comes into its own farther south. It is common in bottomlands from Missouri to Louisiana and eastward, associating with sycamores, silver maples, and willows; indeed, no other birch is found at low altitudes in the southeastern states.

The new branchlets of a river birch are dark shiny red: the red birch. The bark on a young tree is paper thin, flaking into hundreds of pieces that are tinted pinkish-brown: the cinnamon birch. But on an old tree, fifty to ninety feet tall, the bark is thick, deeply fissured, and gray-black, which accounts for the specific name *nigra*: the black birch.

Birches bear male and female flowers in separate catkins on the same tree. The drooping, three-inch-long male catkins of a river birch appear in summer but do not flower until the following spring. The small, upright female catkins produce cone-shaped fruits, an inch and a half long, that ripen and break up after spring floods have receded. Thus the abundant seeds—tiny, two-winged nutlets—have the best chance to germinate, those that aren't quickly consumed by grouse, wild turkeys, songbirds, and rodents.

Because the trunk of a river birch divides low to the ground into two or three large stems, its wood is knotty and of little commercial value. The tree is planted for erosion control and is a popular streetside shade tree in the Pacific Northwest, far beyond its native range. I like it for that flaking cinnamon bark when the tree is in its youth. When it grows old and begins to rot, the cavity-living wild creatures move in—woodpeckers, chickadees, nuthatches, wood ducks, flying squirrels. Perhaps that is the river birch's ultimate purpose on Earth, as an apartment house.

L . L .

Paper Birch

B E T U L A   P A P Y R I F E R A

This is the tree also called canoe birch, or white birch. It is the big, clean white birch which creeps down into our northern states from Canada and reaches up over most of Alaska. It is a large, handsome tree, seventy to even a hundred feet high and with a trunk diameter as great as three feet. In my area it grows to only about half those dimensions.

This was the famous tree whose bark was used by the Indians to make canoes. They made a frame, often of cedar, and then covered it with birch bark sewed together with the long, thin roots of tamarack trees. The seams and sewing-holes were sealed with pitch from pine or balsam. The result was a canoe phenomenally light in weight, beautiful in line and color, and strong enough to carry an Indian and his gear on most rivers and small lakes.

The paper birch looks whiter than any other tree of the family, not only because the bark is actually whiter than the others but because it so often grows near clumps of pines or hemlocks, the deep green of which accentuates the birch's whiteness. The thin, white outer bark often starts to come away from the orange-tinged inner bark, peeling along lines that go around the tree, not up and down. This outer bark is only a little thicker than paper. I have run a strip of it through my typewriter and written on it much as I am writing this manuscript.

The wood is not durable. Cut and left out in the weather, it soon begins to rot. When a paper birch falls in the woodland it is punky within a year or two.

Gray Birch

B E T U L A   P O P U L I F O L I A

The newcomer to the country often mistakes this useful but undistinguished tree for the paper birch. Natives sometimes call it poverty birch. The difference is worth remembering.

Gray birch is a chalky, dirty white, even when it is clean as a fresh cloud in the summer sky. It grows everywhere in the upper Northeast, but particularly in New England. It commonly grows only fifteen or twenty-five feet tall with a trunk diameter of seldom more than nine inches, a foot at most, and it grows in groves, like aspens. Each root sends up several stems, so the gray birches are found in clumps. Short-lived, they are often broken off by summer gales or laden with snow and ice and snapped off in winter. When that happens, new sprouts seem to spring up in a matter of weeks, months at most, from the old roots. Gray birches do not die out easily. Other trees shade them out, in a growing woodland, or men persistently cut them.

There is little call for gray birch wood, except as firewood. I have found it makes better firewood—gives more heat and makes little more smoke—when still green rather than when kept under cover and dry. It is of no use for lumber or posts, and it is too small to be profitably cut for pulpwood.

The gray birch really is a tree for transition land. It moves into abandoned fields, shades and fertilizes them with its leaves, and holds the ground until ash or maple or pine move in and initiate new woodland. Farmers are forever warring with gray birches in their pastures. Small boys swing on them. Woodpeckers mine them for food. They are of slight importance in man's economy, but nature's economy needs them.

Speckled Alder

In speech and in literature, the alders sometimes are confused with the elders, which are cousins of the viburnums and belong to the honeysuckle family. In the field there is no mistaking the one for the other. The alder is usually a shrub, a group of stout stems from a common root, though occasionally it's a small tree with a trunk as much as six inches in diameter and twenty-five or thirty feet high. It has wrinkled leaves broadly ovate in shape and irregularly toothed. It has purple and yellow male catkins about three inches long, and it bears small cones with round-winged seeds that persist on the tree all winter. The elders, in contrast, have flat panicles of white blossoms that mature into heavy heads of dark purple, juicy berries less than a quarter of an inch in diameter.

The alders grow from Maine to Florida and around the Gulf to Texas. They are rare west of Minnesota, though they appear around the Great Lakes. The alder has no value as a timber tree and is not of much use, except as kindling, for firewood. Two West Coast species do grow to timber-size trees, with trunks as much as two feet thick and seventy-five feet high; but we are dealing here with alder bushes, the eastern variety, not alder trees.

Indians used a decoction of alder leaves to treat burns and inflamed wounds. The dried bark was also used for a decoction to check diarrhea, improve circulation, stanch hemorrhage, and ease an upset stomach. An infusion of the bark was used as drops to treat inflamed eyes. And deer and moose love to browse on alder thickets, while birds feast on the seeds.

American Basswood

T I L I A   A M E R I C A N A

When basswood comes to blossom, in late June and early July, the bees assemble, so the clumps of basswood trees are loud as well as fragrant; and in consequence the honeycombs will be full of some of the sweetest honey ever made.

The basswood is a linden, and is so called abroad. Our native basswood is close kin of the famous European shade tree. The name *bass* comes from the word *bast*, or fiber, the reference being to the tough inner bark of the tree, which was long used in making cordage and nets. The wood itself is soft, fine-grained, and easily worked into woodenware and occasionally into furniture.

The strangest thing about the basswood, however, is its flower and fruit. The flowers, small and creamy white and so full of nectar that it literally drips from them, grow on a pendant stem that springs from the center of a leaflike wing. That wing, long and slender and a lighter green than the tree's true leaves, eventually provides a glider for the seed, and thus are new groves of basswood started.

Travel the streams of the hill country of the Northeast and you will find the basswoods. They hug the streambanks, where they make cool, deep shade. The Indians once made canoes from big basswood trunks. Now we make paper pulp from them. Or chopping bowls.

But in midsummer the basswood along our streams is a tree of flowers and fragrance, and we ask no more of it. Dozens of other trees make better timber and better firewood, but where is there another tree that smells so sweet in early July?

Eastern Cottonwood

POPULUS DELTOIDES

This is the familar cottonwood not only of the East but of the Midwest as well. Only as you approach the Rockies does the plains cottonwood appear. The eastern cottonwood is a big, vigorous tree, commonly reaching a hundred feet in height and four feet or more in diameter of trunk. It prefers places where its roots can reach moisture—streambanks, damp valleys, and lakesides.

Staminate and pistillate flowers are borne on separate trees. The flowers bloom in catkins, the males bright yellow, the females deep red. Those catkins may be fat as a man's forefinger and as much as four inches long. The male catkins shed great quantities of pollen. The female catkins ripen seeds and burst pods in midspring, releasing vast numbers of tiny seeds, each with a tuft of cottony floss that acts as a parachute and carries the seed off and away. The leaves are much like aspen leaves but bigger and thicker. Dangling on long, limber stems, they rattle rather than whisper.

Along the road in front of our house, someone long ago planted a row of sugar maples. They are heroic trees, and beautiful. But many years ago, when those maples were young, one of them died and someone put a cottonwood in its place. There it stands today, a huge outsider in that row of maples, overtopping them all, deep red with female catkins in spring—when they fall, as many do, they make the whole road look like the floor of a slaughterhouse—and dropping all its leaves in the fall before a leaf has turned color on the maples. In May, when the seed ripens, that old cottonwood spreads clouds of fluff that comes down the valley like a mist. A strange tree, where it stands, but proud as a white pine.

Quaking Aspen

POPULUS TREMULOIDES

In New England this tree is called a poplar or, more commonly, a popple. Occasionally someone gets fancy and calls it a trembling aspen. Out in Colorado, where I first knew it, it was and still is a quaking aspen, or a quaker. It is one of the most widespread of American poplars, growing from Newfoundland to Alaska, all through New England and the Adirondacks, through the Rocky Mountains and down the Pacific coast into Mexico. In the West it sometimes grows in thickets so dense a man on horseback cannot get through.

It is a small tree, seldom more than forty feet high and fifteen inches through. In some ways it reminds me of the gray birch, though it is a prettier tree with its clean gray-green trunk and its shimmering leaves. It grows rapidly on dry ground, takes over narrow valleys; its leaves turn bright golden tan in October and are shimmering light green again in May. Those leaves are broadly heart-shaped but without a deep notch. Their stems are flattened and thin near the leaf, round and slender near the twig. This allows the leaves to flutter and twist at a mere wisp of a breeze, so they always seem to be trembling, quivering, or quaking, and whispering to each other.

Aspen wood is very pale brown, soft, weak, and not durable when exposed to weather. Larger trees are sometimes sawed and used for interior finish of houses. More often the aspens are cut like hay and fed to the paper mills for pulp. The wood "works" well, so it is also used by craftsmen who make salad bowls and other woodenware.

Black Willow

S A L I X   N I G R A

There are some eighty species of willows found in the United States, according to botanical authorities, and perhaps three hundred species worldwide. In addition, willows tend to crossbreed, so there are hybrids as well—nobody knows how many. Most of our willows tend to grow as low shrubs or large bushes, but some become honest-to-goodness trees. All play an important role in nature by stabilizing the banks of streams and rivers with their fast-spreading and branching root systems.

Male and female blossoms on the willows are borne on separate trees. Insects are the most industrious of the pollinators, but the pollen is very fine and readily windborne. This, of course, helps create those persistent hybrids. We seldom notice the inconspicuous female blossoms. The male blossoms reach their maximum size on the pussy willow, but male catkins on all willows are covered with fuzzy coats after the scales fall and before the stamens "ripen" with pollen.

Black willow is the most common of the big willow trees in the East. It grows along streams and ponds, anywhere there is damp soil. Strangely enough, many streambank willow bushes also are black willows, since the species takes either tree or bush form. As a tree it may have a trunk diameter of three feet and its stems may rise as high as ninety feet. Even in the tree form it usually grows with several main trunks rising from the same root system, as though it had begun to branch at ground level.

Black willow is the only willow I know that has been used for lumber. Before corrugated paper became the standard material for making shipping cases for such grocery items as canned fruit and vegetables, black willow was used for the boxes. It doesn't make good firewood, however, burning quickly and without much heat.

Crack Willow

The crack willow was brought here from England in early Colonial days to provide charcoal for making gunpowder. It throve in New England's climate, and now is found from Quebec to Kentucky and as far west as Kansas and South Dakota. It also is a big tree, up to a hundred feet tall with a trunk as much as six feet in diameter, and it seldom grows as a bush.

Crack willow has lance-shaped leaves three to six inches long. Its bark is gray and deeply furrowed. The shiny twigs are brittle at the base and will snap off in a high wind, which explains both the common and specific names. Unlike the black willow, the crack willow usually grows with a single large trunk that forks several feet above the ground.

Another naturalized willow is the white willow (*Salix alba*), whose wood often is used for baskets and, in England, for cricket bats. To force the growth of basket twigs, willows often were pollarded—limbs cut off and the top removed. Not far from where I live are half a dozen very old willows that obviously were pollarded years ago. I assume they served a basket-maker at one time, though nobody seems to remember him.

For generations, willows were a standard item in the herb doctor's pharmacopoeia. The dried, powdered bark of willow stems was dusted on the navels of newborn children. A mixture of crushed leaves, bark, and stems was used to stanch bleeding. Poultices of mashed roots and leaves were used to ease almost any ache. In Elizabethan England the sap from the willow, when in flower, was believed to be a cure for "films that grow over the eyes"—cataracts, as we know them today. The English also used a solution of boiled willow leaves and twigs, mixed with wine, as a shampoo to eliminate dandruff. And in frontier America, various willow concoctions were used by both whites and Indians to treat venereal disease.

Undoubtedly the curative qualities of willow leaves, stems, and roots come from the presence of salicylic acid in the tree's inner bark. Salicylic acid is the active ingredient in aspirin. However, the botanical name of the genus, *Salix*, does not refer to this. It comes from a Latin word meaning dirty gray and refers to the color of the bark.

Weeping Willow

S A L I X   B A B Y L O N I C A

This is the third tree-size willow in our area, and it never grows as a bush. Like the crack willow, it is an alien, brought to this country in Colonial days as a decorative tree. Its botanical name makes me think of the legendary hanging gardens of ancient Babylon, but the tree actually is a native of China.

We have a weeper here on our farm that was only about three inches in diameter and fifteen feet in height when we came here in 1952. Today it is a massive tree, five feet in diameter at chest height and towering a good seventy-five feet. It has been wracked by wind and storm, has shed truckloads of twigs and branches, and at one time was about to split at its main trunk division ten feet from the ground. Now its huge limbs have been tied to each other with steel cables, it has been trimmed to reduce its top-heavy weight, and its old wounds have healed. It appears to have a long life ahead. Long, that is, as weeping willow life runs, which even in human terms is relatively short.

Like all their relatives, weeping willows thrive near water. They like to get their roots down to a source of moisture that can be tapped constantly. Ours undoubtedly has grown so fast because it sent a taproot down to the water table, which is only about twelve feet down. All willows readily take root when a cutting is thrust into the ground. I once knew a farmer who used willow posts to build a fence across a damp swale. Within five years he had a row of willow trees there because every fencepost took root and grew.

Weeping willows, so far as I know, have no use except as ornamentals. They are beautiful, graceful trees. But they also are "dirty" trees, shedding limbs and twigs in vast quantities every winter. You must love them to put up with them.

Pussy Willow

S A L I X   D I S C O L O R

The pussy willow probably is the best known of all willows, though I have my doubts that one in a dozen people who know the big, gray-furred male catkins would know the bush that bears them if it grew in their own dooryards.

The pussy willow is properly labeled a shrub, though it can be pruned and bullied into the shape of a small tree. The leaves are lance-shaped, pointed at both ends, and about four inches long. The flowers bloom early, in March in my area.

The "pussies" actually are the partly opened male flowers. The bud scales drop off and the silver-furred male catkin appears, big as the last joint of my index finger. This is the pussy, the admired and treasured spring token that, when put in a vase in the living room, makes even a March snow seem definitely transient. Keep this bunch of pussies in that room for ten days, however, and they become full-grown male blossoms. They shed some of the fur and produce stamens tipped with golden-yellow pollen, a ragged-looking bit of florescence but precisely the same as the pussy willow bushes outdoors are about to produce.

On the bush, those male catkins reach the stamen-pollen stage as other bushes produce female blossoms, quite undistinguished, which are ready for pollination. The bees get busy, and the beautiful time of the silvery pussy willow catkins is at an end.

Pussy willows are said to grow best in wet soil, on riverbanks and in such places. Probably so, but we have two pussy willow bushes that thrive in normally dry soil, one at the edge of our vegetable garden.

Persimmon

D I O S P Y R O S   V I R G I N I A N A

I tasted my first wild simmon on a dripping late-October morning. A hard all-night rain had slowed to an on-again, off-again drizzle as we climbed a hill on the Illinois side of the Mississippi River. At the edge of the hilltop woods stood two or three runty persimmon trees with brownish-black bark that was deeply etched into small square plates. A few wrinkled, reddish-orange berries the size of Ping-Pong balls hung from the higher branches, just out of reach. But there were several ripe fruit scattered in the soggy leaf-litter—more than enough for an introduction to this syrup-sweet southern delicacy.

Persimmon is another name we owe to the Algonquian Indians. They collected the fruit, the *pasimenan*, dried them like prunes, and made bread from them all winter. Hill folk call the big berries "possum apples," for on a fall night when the persimmons are ripe you're almost certain to find a passel of fat 'possums gathered for a feast. We humans also have to share the windfall with raccoon, fox, skunk, deer, and just about every other critter of woodland and field with a sweet tooth.

The name for the persimmon genus, *Diospyros*, translates as "fruit of the gods," which is arguably accurate when the berry is fully ripe. But a green persimmon is so laden with astringent tannin that one bite will pucker your lips for an hour. You need to wait until the simmons look and feel like rotten apples, crinkled and mushy, usually after a frost. Separated from the four to eight large, flat seeds, the orange pulp can be used for a variety of delicious cakes, pies, cookies, puddings, jams, and juice.

Persimmons grow as far north as southern New York and Connecticut, west to Kansas and Texas, and south to the Gulf and nearly the tip of Florida. You can find them in old fields, mixed forests, along roadsides and fencerows, and especially in the rich soil of river valleys. The biggest trees, seventy-footers, occur in the bottomlands of the Mississippi and its tributaries. The wood is hard and heavy but has limited use, mostly for the heads of golf clubs.

L . L .

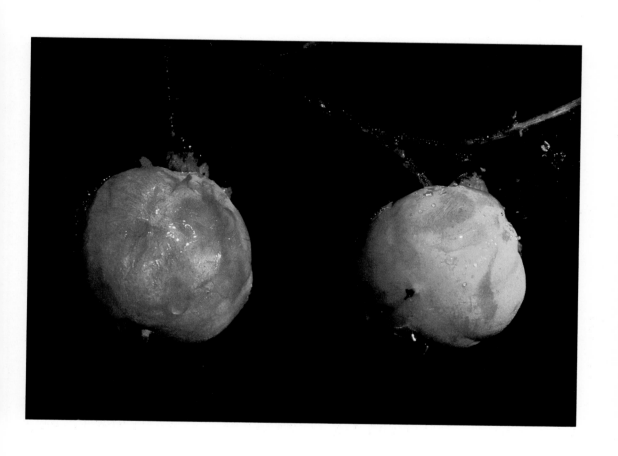

Common Chokecherry

P R U N U S   V I R G I N I A N A

Chokecherries come to bloom in late April, and backcountry roadsides and thin woodlands are warm and pungent with their odor and bright with their white pussytails of blossoms. It's a poor woodland that lacks them, almost anywhere in America, for chokecherries adapt themselves to just about any soil and make small choice among the hills and valleys to an altitude of four thousand feet or more. Our Northeast is full of them.

Only by a liberal stretch of the imagination can the chokecherry be called a fruit tree. It bears cherries that ripen in September, and there are people who make chokecherry jelly. There are even small boys who eat chokecherries, though the cherries are so astringent they pucker the mouth and numb the tongue. And their juice is, in effect, a dye on clothing and fingers. Nobody eats chokecherries for dessert.

The trees, usually small and twisted, are of no commercial value except as firewood. Possibly some early furniture-makers used chokecherry boards now and then, but the larger cherry trees were more favored and provided bigger and better lumber. The tree never amounts to much and often is host to tent caterpillars and other unwelcome pests. It gets scant welcome in well-kept woods.

Yet it persists, thanks to the birds that eat the cherries and plant the seeds along fences and in the woods. It thrives where more valuable trees give up. It is a weed tree. But in May, when it's in bloom, it is full of beauty and pungent fragrance—and bees. Perhaps that is its reason for being.

Black Cherry

P R U N U S   S E R O T I N A

Some people call this rum cherry and others call it whiskey cherry. Some who have seen black cherry bowls I turned on my lathe called it mahogany, and they weren't the first to make that mistake. Early American furniture made of black cherry has passed for mahogany time and again. The two woods are much alike in color and grain, but mahogany shows pores visible to the naked eye, and cherry doesn't.

Time was when our woodlands were full of wild black cherry trees, which often grew to noble size, a hundred feet in height, four to five feet in girth. The astringent fruit was used to make a beverage called cherry bounce, with the help of rum or brandy which somewhat tempered the bitterness. That juice is still used to flavor some alcoholic beverages. The essence of bitter almond, or prussic acid, in the leaves and bark is used as as astringent in medicines and in treatments for sore throat.

Cherry wood, because it does not tend to warp or split, is useful in cabinetwork and often used to make coffins. Daniel Boone is said to have made several cherry coffins for himself, but he gave them all away except the last one.

A friend of ours up here in the hills had to cut a good-size cherry tree to make room for a new driveway, so he took it to a sawmill, had it cut into planks, seasoned them, and gave me enough to turn a set of salad bowls, of which I spoke at the beginning. The wood turns perfectly on a lathe, and the bowls are beautiful to see on the table.

Fire Cherry

PRUNUS PENSYLVANICA

The wild cherries were heavy with fruit the last time I hiked the old logging trails in the Huron Mountains of Michigan's Upper Peninsula. There were chokecherries dropping from their burden of half-inch black berries. But mostly there were fire cherries ablaze with clusters of tiny, bright red fruit. They lined both sides of the rocky path I followed toward what the topographic map showed was a waterfall on the Yellow Dog River, one of the UP's famous trout streams. But I was after pictures, not brookies.

Fire cherry, or pin cherry as others call it, is a pioneer species on forest lands that have been clear-cut or swept by fire. The pure stands of fire cherry that follow such devastation provide protection, in cover and shade, for the seedlings of the trees that will replace the original forest. And the fruit feed a horde of birds and animals—including, as was freshly evident that autumn afternoon black bears.

Every few yards along the trail were steaming piles of bear dung filled with cherry pits. Here and there, cherry trees with trunks as thick as a sumo wrestler's thigh were broken to the ground. A black bear can, when it wishes, daintily pick berries one at a time. But autumn is a busy time in the bear's life, and it takes a lot of little cherries to fill its caloric needs. So the bear usually gobbles leaves, twigs, and fruit with one fast sweep of the paw, letting its digestive system sort things out. To reach fruit at the top of a small tree, the bear straddles the trunk and rides it to the ground.

Up ahead a tree splintered with a sharp c-r-a-c-k. Armed only with a telephoto lens, I tiptoed around a bend in the trail. The broken upper limbs of a fire cherry hung over the path. The trunk was deeply gouged, and the leaves rattled like those of a quaking aspen in a gale. Only there wasn't a breath of breeze. And in a gravelly washout, grains of sand slid into paw prints of awesome proportions.

I bet that waterfall on the Yellow Dog would have made a pretty picture.

L . L .

Mountain-ash

SORBUS SPP.

In Europe, and sometimes here, this is known as the rowan-tree. References to it reach far back in English literature.

Mountain-ash has no relationship to the ash trees. It belongs to the huge rose family, cousin of shadbush, pear, apple, chokeberry, as well as all the thorns, the plums, and the cherries. It has smooth bark, alternate compound leaves, and flat-topped panicles of small, creamy-white flowers.

But it is the fruit that marks the mountain-ash definitively. Those panicles of blossoms become spectacular flat-topped panicles of brilliant orange-red berries, a color unmistakable in the woodland. In autumn the leaves turn a bright, clean gold color, but they soon fall. Then the berries glow, demanding attention. They really are miniature pomes, tiny apples about a quarter of an inch in diameter.

Our native mountain-ash (*Sorbus americana*) is largely found in the upper Great Lakes, the Northeast, and from Ontario to Newfoundland, but it sneaks south along the high ridges of the Appalachians. European mountain-ash (*Sorbus aucuparia*) is widely planted as an ornamental tree as well as along superhighways in the East, perhaps to divert drivers' attention from the suicidal maniacs in the other cars. It has become widely naturalized, from Alaska to Canada and the northern states.

The mountain-ash berries have a sharp, unpleasant acid flavor. Birds eat them eagerly, especially grouse. The berries seem to have the same astringent substance as the bark of the small tree. And this bark once was used in place of quinine, in the remote settlements, to treat malaria. Anything with that astringent a flavor, it was believed, must be good for the health. Moose eagerly eat the inner bark, which is supposed to be less vigorously flavored.

Serviceberry

A M L A N C H I E R   A R B O R E A

I have also known this shrub or tree as juneberry, shadblow, shadbush, and sarvisberry. It is another cousin of the apple. Because it blooms about the time the shad run upstream from the sea to spawn, it was named shadblow or shadbush by early settlers. I've heard it said, though this is disputed, that it is known in the southern mountains as serviceberry or sarvisberry because it blooms at a time when the preacher-man makes his springtime trip up to the remote hollows and holds religious services for those who died or were born or took up living together since his last seasonal visit.

It isn't much of a tree, even when it grows to tree size, though I have seen specimens with a trunk a foot through and a height of twenty-five feet. Usually it grows as a tall, gangly shrub, reaching up for sunlight from among the real trees in the moist woodland. We have several striking examples of it here along our river. Down at the Big Bend is one that shines like a Christmas tree when it blooms. Along the road just beyond our old milkhouse is one that seems to be full of small white butterflies when in bloom. On a stone pier in the middle of the river, left standing when the branch line of the railroad was dismantled, stands a shadblow now ten feet high and shapely as a Christmas tree. In April, when it blooms, we walk up the road to stand and look at it, one of the most beautiful trees we know.

Shadblow berries are dry and pleasantly tasty, but they are hard to get. The birds love them. Shadblow wood makes good tool handles and once was used for lance shafts by the Indians. I think of this every time I speak its Latin name—*Amlanchier*.

Apple

MALUS SYLVESTRIS

Across the creek and up the hill, at the edge of my little woodlot, grows an apple tree of undetermined age, origin, and genetics. It has had no care for generations, if ever: its lower branches are mostly dead, and its trunk is divided in two by a white ash tree that grows straight as a ship's mast. Yet it still produces apples, at least a few bushels every year, a bumper crop every now and then.

Those apples are yellow with a blush of pink, smallish, hard and tart, blotched and wormy, generally unfit for human consumption. But the deer don't mind. In September and October the grass of my meadow is criss-crossed by whitetail highways that lead to the base of that old apple tree, and flattened where the deer, satiated from their gluttony, have bedded down to sleep.

The original apple came from Eurasia. I say "original" because in North America alone, some three thousand varieties of apples have been developed by cultivation or accidental hybridization since the first colonists dropped sail on these shores.

Commercial apples today are grown for appearance and hardiness, not for taste. Apples in the supermarkets are large, perfectly shaped, beautiful to look at, unblemished and unbruised, and available year-round. But they have a skin so hard it is indigestible, and the flesh is about as delicious as the paper in this book.

Few farmers grow the great, flavorful varieties of yesteryear, apples with names like winter banana, strawberry, sheepnose, twenty ounce, pound sweet, Grimes golden, orange pippin—or Roxbury russet. We're told these old-timers require too much care, do not last long enough, have few uses, take too many years to bear fruit, are susceptible to disease.

Properly pruned and sprayed and nurtured, that "wild" apple tree across the creek and up the hill might be coaxed into producing fine fruit, of one of those forgotten varieties. But then I'd have to compete with the deer for the crop, and they're here seven days a week.

L . L .

Honeylocust

GLEDITSIA TRIACANTHOS

The honeylocust is not a native of my area, but it grows here and thrives. Down the road from our farm there is a grove of honeylocusts that probably sprang from seeds produced by a big old locust tree on a farm almost half a mile away. And on our own mountain we have a locust grove, up above the field of white pines, that must have been there at least fifty years. Maybe it, too, came from that big locust down the road. But that happens often and in many places. There probably are as many locusts in cultivation today as there are growing wild, and all of them produce seeds.

I respect the locust trees, not for their shapely form and solid timbers but for their thorns. I have heard that not even gray squirrels will climb a honeylocust because of the thorns, and I must admit that I never saw a squirrel in any of the locusts I know. Those thorns grow on the trunk and branches as well as on the twigs, and they are needle-sharp and often three-pronged. Sometimes they are several inches long.

Locust leaves are compound, sometimes with twenty or more leaflets to the stem. There is no terminal leaflet. The flowers are small, greenish, and in pendant clusters. The fruit is a shiny, leathery reddish-brown pod ten to fifteen inches long, with small, hard, beanlike seeds inside. The pods twist as they ripen, and eventually the twist sets up tensions that split the pod and hurl the seeds a considerable distance. Since the pods also have a sweetish inner lining, various animals eat them and thus distribute the seeds.

Honeylocust wood is hard and durable, though of little commercial use. Indians once made their bows of honeylocust wood.

Black Locust

R O B I N I A   P S E U D O A C A C I A

It stormed early last June when the black locusts were in full flower, a real Wagnerian episode with ominous clouds, deafening thunder, and blinding lightning. Had this been my native Michigan, I would have gathered the kids and cats and run for the basement. But tornadoes are rare indeed in these parts, so I watched the grand show from the front door until the gale-driven deluge washed everything from view.

When the *sturm und drang* was over, I drove around to check the damage. But down the road several huge trees were flattened, mostly shallow-rooted willows, and broken power lines snapped about.

Then I turned into a narrow lane, lined on both sides with locust trees, and skidded to a stop, awestruck. For two hundred yards the pavement was covered with a half-inch of snow. Only the "snow," on inspection, turned out to be a carpet of creamy-white petals from the pea-flowers of the black locust, a carpet laid down by that afternoon's gullywasher. Those fragrant, five-petaled flowers hang in loose clusters ten to fourteen inches long, bloom in late May and June, and attract swarms of bees which make a particularly delicious honey from their nectar.

Like honeylocust, a cousin in the vast legume family, black locust does not belong in New England. Its natural range follows the core of the Appalachians from Pennsylvania to Alabama, then jumps over the Mississippi to the Ozarks. But how does one define *belong*? The mockingbird and opossum aren't native here, either, but both southerners have settled in comfortably.

Virginia Indians, who made bows of the tree's tough wood, were the first to plant black locust and expand its range. Colonists cut locust cornerposts for their cabins. The trees grow like weeds, to a height of sixty feet, and became popular for shelterbelts and as ornamentals, though their feathery foliage offers little shade. Today the black locust is found from Maine to California, delighting bees and the birds and squirrels who harvest the beanlike seeds in its flattened, four-inch-long pods.

L . L .

Flowering Dogwood

CORNUS FLORIDA

We once lived near a hillside covered with a thin woodland that had a liberal number of dogwoods in its understory growth. Every May, before the big trees had fully leafed out, that hillside was a magic place that appeared to be filled with white butterflies. The dogwood bloomed, and those white blossoms were there until the leaves were fully opened and the dogwoods were lost in the shade. And every October that hillside was busy with squirrels eating those dogwoods' fat red berries.

Dogwood is a native tree, and it comes with both white and pink flowers. It is a small tree, seldom as tall as twenty-five feet here in the North. It grows with long, reaching branches that turn upward at the tips, and when the flowers bloom they seem to be in layers on the tree. Botanists point out that the big white "petals" of the blossom actually are sepals, not petals at all, and that the real blossoms are those inconspicuous clustered florets in the center. That is a technicality, for those white sepals, sometimes making a flower four inches across, are what makes the flower notable. In early autumn a small cluster of bright red berries ripen where the flower appeared, and birds and squirrels assemble and feast.

The name *dogwood* comes from the old word *dag*, meaning a skewer to hold meat together, and the wood was used for skewers at one time. The wood, tougher than hickory, has long been used to make heads for golf clubs as well as chisel handles, mallet heads, wedges, small pulleys, knitting needles, and spindles and shuttles for weavers.

Red-Osier Dogwood

CORNUS STOLONIFERA

Two signs of spring are infallible: the golden-amber look of the willow stems and the blood-red livening of the red-osier dogwood stems.

This dogwood shrub—it may reach a height of eight feet or so, but usually is no more than five or six—grows in clumps and clusters along streambanks and in other damp, sandy lowlands. Its leaves are a light olive green, strongly ribbed and with the veins converging toward the tip in typical dogwood fashion. The blossoms come in June and are in flat clusters of yellowish-white, four-petaled flowers about a quarter of an inch across. These flowers mature into dull gray berries about the size of small peas, each on a red stem.

That is the mark of this dogwood—the red stems. The plant's main stems are red with white or grayish dots scattered over them. The leaf stems are red. The flower and fruit stems are red. And, as I said, this red livens to a point where one could almost believe blood was pulsing through all those stems when the first turn to spring is at hand.

This dogwood grows over most of the eastern United States north of Washington, D.C., then westward to the Pacific, down through the Southwest, and up all the way into Alaska. In the West the Indians ate the berries, used the wood to make bows, and brewed a decoction of the leaves and bark to treat colds and malarial fevers. With fat added, this decoction made a useful ointment.

Common Winterberry

ILEX VERTICILLATA

This northern version of holly is also called black alder, probably because its leaves turn brownish-black in the autumn, and because it grows in damp places, like alder. But instead of the conelike fruits the alders bear, the winterberry has clusters of beautiful red berries about a quarter of an inch in diameter, berries much like those on Christmas holly. The berries tend to remain on the bushes all winter.

This is a shrub, though occasionally it grows to as much as twenty feet in height with one principal stem. Normally it is six or eight feet high and has several stems from the same root. It grows as underbrush among the trees along slow-flowing brooks or on the margins of ponds. Its bark is gray, and its branches tend to reach upward.

We find winterberry all along a brook that flows into one of our nearby glacial ponds, where we go to gather marsh-marigold greens in the spring. The marsh-marigolds leaf out and come to bloom, with their big golden-buttercup flowers, before the winterberry leaves are fully out. The winterberry flowers are inconspicuous, very small and white. They don't appear until June or early July.

The shrub's leaves are elliptical and abruptly pointed, dark green in color and with small teeth around the edges; some of the plants seem to have no teeth at all on the leaves. There is no resemblance to the leaves of Christmas holly, with their sharp spines. Christmas, or American, holly, by the way, grows on Cape Cod and in other places along the coast from there southward. It cannot survive our severe inland winters.

American Bladdernut

S T A P H Y L E A   T R I F O L I A

There was this clump of bushes on the hillside that caught my eye. I still do not know quite why, but something about their deep green compound leaves, three to a stem, made me watch them. It was our first spring here, a good many years ago, and we were still learning about our trees and flowers. These bushes had leaves something like those on the pear tree at the edge of the vegetable garden, but not as thick and leathery. And as I said, these were compound, three to the stem.

They came to bloom in May, inconspicuous bloom, small whitish flowers with five petals. These little flowers appeared in drooping clusters at the base of the leaves. Looking at those flowers, so unimportant, so readily over-looked, I dismissed the bushes, forgot them.

Nothing special happened all summer. Nothing to watch, at least. I was more interested in the bayberries, the shrub dogwoods, the viburnums. Then in September I looked at those bushes again and saw strange pods on them—pods, from those unimportant little flowers. These pods were about an inch long, big around as my thumb, divided into three segments, and they were still green. I let them ripen till they turned tan and papery, then picked a few. Inside the papery pods were several round, dark, hard seeds. The riper pods were already beginning to open, from the top. A good wind would flip the branches and toss the seeds of this strange bush, the bladdernut.

Horsechestnut

A E S C U L U S   H I P P O C A S T A N U M

One account says this tree got its common name because the nuts at one time were fed to horses and were used as medicine for them. Maybe so, but the horses I have known would not willingly eat them, they are so bitter. The belief goes far back, for the name is there in the scientific identification of Linnaeus's time. The tree is also called a buckeye, and I prefer that. The tree's nut does look something like a big buck's reddish-brown eye.

It is a beautiful tree and is often used ornamentally. It came originally from Turkey, was taken to England by the Crusaders, and was brought here much later. We have several native buckeyes, none of them as beautiful as the imported one, which has spread from cultivation and is often found in the woodland, especially in the Midwest. Here in my area there are several specimens, all of them planted by admirers who wanted them as dooryard trees.

They have compound leaves, normally seven leaflets arranged radially, each about the size and shape of a black ash leaf. The flowers, which come in June, make the tree unmistakable. They are showy white and come in erect clusters, the whiteness of the petals accentuated by dull yellow and madder-purple spots. The fruit is in a pod with rather soft spines and is a large, shining chestnut-red nut. It matures in September, looks like a large true chestnut, but the meat is bitter and inedible.

Sugar Maple

ACER SACCHARUM

The maples have sweetened our lives, literally. From the sugar maple came the pioneers' sugar, and still comes the best of all natural syrups. The maple's lumber provided floors that withstood the traffic of human feet for centuries. It provided some of the most beautiful furniture, and most durable chairs and tables, ever made. The trees themselves, largely free from disease or pests, have shaded dooryards and streets ever since there were settlements in America. And in autumn the maples have made the celebration of the color a twice-beautiful spectacle all across the land, with their flaming reds, their spectacular golden yellows, and all the shades between.

Sap rises early in the sugar maple, some years as early as Washington's Birthday. Sap-rise doesn't mean that spring is here, however. It means that we have a succession of mild days and chilly nights, which can end any time but which also proves that spring is on its way. The sugar maples respond to temperature, length of daylight, angle of the sun, and whatever other mysterious factors prompt the processes that lead to blossom and leaf in due time.

Sugar of a sort can be made from birches and several other species of trees, but that of the maples is best and that from the sugar maple is best of all. Sugar made from the sap of silver maples, for instance, looks and tastes much the same as that from sugar maples, but it contains enough tannic acid to turn tea black. In the Midwest, some pioneers made sugar from the sap of the boxelder, or ashleaf maple, but it had an acid taste and required much more sap to make a pound of sugar.

The sugar maple is a magnificent tree and it grows over a considerably greater range than the rather limited maple-sugar area. It is found and flourishes as far south as Georgia and as far west as Nebraska; but south of Virginia it doesn't produce sugar, probably a result of the climate.

The enduring glory of the tree is its shape and shade in summer, its color in autumn, and its sap and sugar in spring.

Striped Maple

A C E R   P E N S Y L V A N I C U M

Another name for this big shrub, or small tree, is moosewood, but the one most fully descriptive is goosefoot maple. The leaves, with one point and two pointed lobes, are almost exactly like a big goose's foot in outline. But the bark, which usually is smooth, is ruddy brown with greenish-white stripes up and down the trunk.

This is one of the smaller maples, seldom more than twenty-five feet high even when it takes the tree form. Usually it is a scraggly, tall bush with several stems rising from the same root. Its flowers appear in early June, after the tree or shrub has leafed out. The flowers are green, inconspicuous. They mature into typical maple samaras with the two seeds joined but the wings spread wide apart. The fruit is green and continues green until autumn, hanging in clusters from the ends of the twigs.

Striped maple is abundant in Maine and westward into Minnesota, south along the Allegheny Mountains all the way to Georgia. Though abundant in western Massachusetts, it is uncommon in other parts of New England.

It has no commercial use that I know of, though its sap, like that of all maples, does have a sugar content. The bushes seldom grow to a size where any of the trunks could be tapped.

I find it interesting that this shrub, or tree, is still called moosewood in my area, even by the old-timers. Undoubtedly this means that moose were native to this area at one time, perhaps around 1700, though they haven't been here within the memory of old men still living.

Red Maple

A C E R R U B R U M

This tree is often called swamp maple, but to me it is forever the red maple simply because there is a valley across the way and down the road that is full of red maples, a damp valley that is not quite a swamp. And every September, when it is time for the color to start in this area, I go there and see that color coming. I see it first, of course, in the sumac along the road-sides everywhere. But that is only the spark that sets fire to those low-land maples.

The color begins with a few red leaves on a few branches. It spreads, much as a fire spreads, from leaf to leaf and branch to branch, and it deepens from a pinkish-red to a cherry red to a full crimson red. And by then the whole valley is afire with those soft maples. It is spectacular. It is something one must see to believe. And after that the hillside beyond is in red and yellow and orange flames, as the color spreads upward from those red maples, to the sugar maples, to the gray birch, to the wild cherry and the sweet birch, and finally to the oaks. But it starts down there in the damp valley, with those red maples.

In the spring we have the same thing, but on a far smaller scale. The red maples come to bud and blossom, red as wine, and the first tiny leaves appear, red as the blood-red flowers. The stems are red. The whole effect is flushed, beautiful in a restrained way. And after the red maples, the sugar maples bloom, downright pale, almost unnoticed.

Red maple is the most widespread of all our maples. Pioneers used its bark in dying, to produce a blue color, and they used the wood for turning all kinds of lathe work. It has little market as lumber.

Silver Maple

ACER SACCHARINUM

Canoeing the Meramec River in the Missouri Ozarks on a late October afternoon, I was puzzled by the unfamiliar maple trees that battled with sycamores for growing space on the floodplain. It was their graceful, distinctive leaves that caught my attention. Their five lobes were deeply cut, and compared with the brilliant crimsons, oranges, and golds of northern upland maples in autumn, they were virtually colorless—a pale greenish-yellow.

"Soft maple," responded my paddle-mate in answer to my question. The answer didn't help. Sugar maple, I knew, is sometimes called hard maple, or rock maple, because of its durable, close-grained wood. But so is the closely related black maple. Common names for trees are something of a problem. Ornithologists have an official committee to approve both vernacular and scientific names for birds. But botanists have no such august court, and a single tree species may be known by several common names. Perhaps that is why botanists always talk in Latin and Greek, although I sometimes suspect it is also to impress the laity.

But "soft maple" struck no familiar chord, and my field guide was packed away. So I had to wait until we set up camp to identify the silver maple, a common tree of riverbottoms and swamps from New Brunswick to Florida and west to the prairies. Those cutleaves are silvery-white beneath, accounting for the name; and while the wood is not really soft, it is brittle and inferior, useful only for packing crates and the cheapest furniture.

The silver maple has the largest winged seeds of any native maple, up to three inches long. Squirrels and grosbeaks love them. Though it is a fast-growing species, reaching a mature height of eighty to ninety feet in less than a century, it has a short, stout trunk up to three feet through, few large forks, a ragged crown, and is not considered "pleasing" in form. But on a fresh morning after a night-long rain, with the sun struggling to pierce the fog shrouding the tangled bottomlands, it is the perfect tree for the place.

L . L .

160

Boxelder

ACER NEGUNDO

This is the poor relation of the maple family, the country cousin that has soft-shelled beetles in its hair. Its common name makes no mention of its distinguished kinship, though botanists and others of scientific bent do speak of it as the ashleaf maple, or *Acer negundo*. But that doesn't repair its reputation. It grows all over the Northeast, over the mountains into the Midwest, and far out across the Great Plains. It has its virtues.

One of those virtues is its seeds, which ripen in the usual maple form as samaras, or keys, each containing a fat nutlike seed with a broad, flat wing. These seeds are borne in bunches that hang like light tan tassels after the leaves have fallen. Each autumn they festoon the trees, and there they are all winter, providing nutritious handouts to hungry birds and squirrels. Even the gluttonous evening grosbeaks will eat them after they have eaten all the free-lunch sunflower seeds in sight.

There is no hint of the maple in this tree's leaves, which are compound, each leaflet something like an ash leaf. Its sap is faintly sweet and can be boiled down to second-rate sugar. Its wood is of little value except as firewood. But it is a friendly tree. It grows quickly. And those winter tassels of seeds on the female trees—this is the only maple that is not bisexual—give it a generous, handsome look. In a country-cousin sort of way.

Poison Ivy

RHUS RADICANS

If there is a purpose for poison ivy in the big pattern it must be to teach people to be wary not only of what they see but of what they "know."

There was a young teacher from the city in her first job, teaching first grade in a small-town school. She had taken a quick course in "nature study" and led her whole class to a nearby woodland to gather colorful autumn leaves. The youngsters collected maple leaves, but she took yellow and orange leaves from a vine she called woodbine. Within a week she and half the class, inflamed and swollen, itching miserably, learned the difference between woodbine and poison ivy. (The leaves of woodbine or Virginia creeper come in fives, those of poison ivy in threes. Ivy leaves are shiny, oily-looking; woodbine leaves are not oily.)

Another novice to the country, a back-to-nature person, gathered poison ivy berries, which are gray when ripe (woodbine berries are grape purple), mistaking them for bayberries, and tried to boil wax from them to make candles. She, too, learned the hard way.

Poison ivy grows either as a vine, which sometimes climbs high into a tree, or as a low, spreading bush. It often is found on old stone walls in New England. The leaves are compound, three leaflets to a cluster, all toothless, smooth, and with that sleek, oily look mentioned above. The flowers are small, in clusters and dull greenish-white. The berries are lusterless gray and about the size of BB shot.

Poison ivy and jewelweed often grow in the same damp, lowland areas. Jewelweed stems are full of watery juice that neutralizes the poison of the ivy for many persons. Learn to recognize both plants and you may save yourself some pain and trouble.

Smooth Sumac

RHUS GLABRA

In earlier days, sumac leaves, bark, and even roots were gathered to be used in dying and tanning. European sumac is still used that way along the Mediterranean. And in Asia there is a sumac whose seed yields an oil that can be made into candles and a juice that makes a natural varnish for lacquerwork. If sumac were less common here, if it demanded care and pampering, it probably would be cherished and admired simply for its own beauty.

But sumac is a weed. It invades pastures and shades out the grass. It crowds out tree seedlings and bushes along the riverbank. It crowds country roadsides. It is stubborn and persistent, wherever it strikes root. We have to fight it, year after year, at the lower end of our vegetable garden.

Some people gather the sumac berries and make an iced drink from them; it tastes vaguely like lemonade. The Indians used a cold infusion of the berries for fever, colds, and diarrhea and used it as a gargle. The seeds were dried and powdered and used to halt hemorrhaging. Juice of the roots was believed to remove warts.

But, aside from holding the soil against riverbank floods, sumac is primarily a shrub to be admired for its own beauty, particularly from late summer till early winter. It turns color early, and its reds and oranges are brilliant. It sets an example for the whole woodland, for its color is something only maple and gum and dogwood can equal.

Poison Sumac

TOXICODENDRON VERNIX

All the sumacs, and poison ivy as well, belong to the cashew family. But don't let that fool you into looking for cashew nuts among them, and especially into too close contact with the small tree sometimes called poison-dogwood. Why it is called dogwood, I have no idea, for it is a sumac: It has the sumac's compound leaves, and its flowers and fruit are almost identical with those of poison ivy, a close cousin of the sumacs.

Poison sumac grows in low, damp places and usually becomes a shrub rather than a tree. Occasionally, though, it grows as a tree as much as twenty feet high, with a short, stout trunk that forks early and spreads into a round-topped head. The leaves, like staghorn sumac leaves, are compound, with as many as thirteen leaflets, smooth, elliptical in shape, lusterless light green in color. All parts of this plant are poisonous to the touch, and even the smoke from burning the branches carries enough of the oily irritant to give a bystander a case of poisoning on the face or hands.

This noxious shrub is supposed to be found only infrequently in southern New England, and then in damp places along the seacoast. But there just happens to be at least one small tree of this species growing healthily beside a pathway in the cemetery at Canaan, Connecticut, in a relatively dry place and about seventy-five miles from the nearest shoreline. How it got there, I have no idea. The late Aretas Saunders, a bird-song authority who often visited that spot looking for birds, pointed it out to me.

White Ash

This tree is also called American ash, and with reason. It is a kind of all-American tree, growing almost everywhere east of the Rocky Mountains. It is also used by most Americans, for sports equipment—baseball bats, tennis racquet frames, hockey sticks, bowling alley floors, oars, polo mallets—as well as for tool handles and porch furniture. And to top all this, it is a beautiful tree.

We have, here on our acres, a clump of white ash trees near the small waterfall where our Springhouse Brook makes its final drop from the mountainside to the middle pasture. I watch those trees every year to see what color they will turn when autumn comes. Occasionally they simply turn a warm bronzed yellow, but more often they go through a stage of purplish-blue before turning to mauve and bronze. And then they fall, and those special colors, like nothing else in the woodland, are gone for another year. When they assume that purple shade I still blink my eyes and wonder if I am imagining things. But others see the same color there, so it must be true.

In earlier times, before the lumbermen had cut most of the really big specimens of our trees, white ash occasionally grew to heroic dimensions, as much as a hundred and seventy-five feet tall and five feet in diameter. In the deep, rich soil of the Midwest it still grows more than a hundred feet tall, with its branches spreading and the compound leaves, usually with seven leaflets, clustered toward the branch ends. You can stand under such a tree, well in the shade, and look up and see the sky.

Black Ash

F R A X I N U S   N I G R A

The black ash is a northern tree, seldom found south of southeastern New England but growing freely northward into Canada and west beyond Lake Superior. It prefers wetlands, stream borders, and cool swamplands. It is a tall, slender tree, its branches reaching upward rather than outward, as do those of the white ash. In the autumn its leaves have no spectacular color variation. The black ash simply turns a rusty brown and then, one chilly morning, all its leaves seem to fall at once.

It used to be called hoop ash or basket ash. Its wood can be split quite easily, if you know the trick, into thin, tough splints. The old basket-makers were masters of this trick. Thirty years ago I knew one of them down at Pound Ridge, Connecticut, a village that got its name, tradition says, from the fact that black ash was pounded there to make those splints for the basketmakers. The old man I knew said he went out into the woods, chose his trees, had them cut into billets, let the billets season to exactly the right point, then pounded them with special mauls. At a certain stage of pounding, the layers of wood began to separate at the annual growth rings. Then he took those splints and soaked them in water and wove them into baskets. We have four or five of those baskets, among the best we ever saw. I use one, which the maker called a clam basket, for my desk wastebasket.

The black ash looks a good deal like the white ash except that it is taller and more slender. Its compound leaves have more leaflets, as many as eleven. Its samaras are notched at the tip.

Elderberry

The elderberry is a graceful, beautiful bush that might have become a decorative shrub for neatly clipped lawns. But it didn't. It is a wildling loved by the birds, so heavy-headed with fruit that it sometimes breaks its own stems, and considered a weed by neat gardeners. Its fruit is too bitter to be eaten raw and too sweet to jell without added pectin, but it does make a good wine that is reputed to have medicinal qualities.

Elderberry bushes grow seven or eight feet high, sometimes twice that. They like moist lowlands and grow in thickets. They are found from Nova Scotia to Florida and west to Kansas and Texas. The branches are dark maroon or green, and they give off a rank odor when crushed. The leaves are compound, with usually seven acutely pointed ovate leaflets to the stem. The flowers are creamy white and bloom in broad, flat-topped clusters. The fruit, small purplish-black berries full of juice when ripe, matures in September, also in those broad, flat-topped clusters. The leaves give off that same rank odor when crushed.

Elderberry branches are pithy and for many years they were used to make spiles for collecting maple sap. They were cut into six-inch lengths, the pith was forced out of them, and they were driven into the holes bored through the bark of the sap trees. A neighbor of ours who wanted to make syrup "the old way" used elderberry spiles a few years ago, boiled the sap in an open tub, and learned how much sap it takes to make a gallon of syrup. How much? Well, close to forty gallons.

Highbush Blueberry

VACCINIUM CORYMBOSUM

It is easy to get lost in the blueberry thickets and not know whether you are dealing with blueberries, huckleberries, dangleberries, farkleberries, or bilberries. These are not regional names, either. But the two most often confused, really, are blueberries and huckleberries. I think I can distinguish between them, but only by the fruit. Their leaves and blossoms, to my eye at least, are very much alike. But huckleberries are so dark purple they look black and they have little or no "bloom." Blueberries are a trace lighter in color and do have the whitish bloom. Blueberries have few seeds. Huckleberries seem, by contrast, to be quite seedy. Most blueberries are sweeter than huckleberries.

All these members of the family prefer an acid soil. They take over when an oak woodland has been cut or otherwise removed, the blueberry roots working their way down through the leathery oak leaves, which decay very slowly, and into the acid soil beneath. In fact, these blueberry—or huckleberry—tangles sometimes are so thick and so stubborn that they keep any other bushes from getting a foothold. On some of our mountains in this area, where the oaks were cut a couple of generations ago for timbers and for charcoal, there are blueberry thickets a man cannot force his way through.

Blueberries, huckleberries, and all the rest have leathery, smooth-edged, ovoid leaves, cylindrical flowers quite small, only about a quarter of an inch long, and dark blue or purple berries from a quarter to half an inch in diameter. Highbush blueberry grows ten or twelve feet tall, under the best conditions; some of the southern species are evergreen.

Bush Honeysuckle

DIERVILLA LONICERA

This is probably the most common of our native honeysuckles. It grows from Newfoundland west to Michigan and Wisconsin, south down the uplands to Georgia. It prefers the dry, rocky hillsides the eastern mountains provide and is a part of the underbrush of most of the woodlands of New England and the whole Northeast.

It is a relatively small bush, seldom as much as five feet high. Its stems are usually covered with smooth brown bark, though in older specimens the bark may be scaly. The leaves are lance-shaped, shallow-toothed, and deep green. The flowers are honey-colored, funnel-shaped, about three-fourths of an inch long and divided into five lobes, each flower having five rather long stamens. The flowers commonly occur in clusters of three either at the twig tips or at the junction of leaf and stem. The fruit is an oblong capsule with a slightly beaked tip.

The flowers are odorless, at least to the human nose. But the bees find them attractive and swarm to them when they open. Later in the season, when the fruit has ripened, the birds move in and eat the berries.

Honeysuckle leaves were boiled by the Indians to make a decoction that was used as a remedy for sore throats and coughs. Probably the warm liquid was soothing, whether it had any healing quality or not.

Index of Common Names

Index of Scientific Names

A Note About the Author

Hal Borland was born in Nebraska, grew up in Colorado, and lived in New England from 1945 until his death in 1978. He is the author of more than thirty books—including the classic *When the Legends Die*; his memoirs, *High, Wide and Lonesome*; and two recent favorites, *Hal Borland's Book of Days* and *Hal Borland's Twelve Moons of the Year*. He was for many years a contributing editor of *Audubon* magazine. In 1942, he wrote the first of the "outdoor editorials" that became an institution in the Sunday edition of the *New York Times*. Mr. Borland received many honors and awards, among them the John Burroughs Nature Award in 1968 for *Hill Country Harvest*. His wife, author Barbara Dodge Borland, still lives on their 100-acre Connecticut farm beside the Housatonic River in the lower Berkshires.

A Note About the Photographer

Les Line has been the editor of *Audubon*, the magazine of the National Audubon Society, since 1966. He is also a noted nature photographer, and his pictures have appeared in many books and national magazines. His byline, as photographer, editor, or author, appears on twenty-one books. He is a Fellow of the Rhode Island School of Design, and in 1981 he was awarded an honorary degree of Doctor of Literature from Bucknell University. Born in Sparta, Michigan, Les Line began his journalism career at the age of twelve, writing sports stories and taking pictures for local newspapers. As a reporter in Midland, Michigan, he won many awards for news photography and conservation writing. Mr. Line lives with his wife and two children in Dobbs Ferry, New York. They have a country retreat in Dutchess County, "just over the hills" from the Borland farm in adjacent Connecticut.

A Note on the Type

The text of this book was set in Weiss, a typeface designed in Germany by Emil Rudolf Weiss (1875–1942). The design of the roman was completed in 1928 and that of the italic in 1931. Both are well balanced and even in color, reflecting the subtle skill of a fine calligrapher.

Composition by Heritage Printers, Inc., Charlotte, North Carolina
Separations by Toppan Printing Company (America), Inc., New York, New York
Printing by American Printers and Lithographers, Chicago, Illinois
Binding by A. Horowitz & Sons, Fairfield, New Jersey

Design by Dorothy Schmiderer